The
(Other)
F
Word

The (Other) F Word

A CELEBRATION OF THE FAT & FIERCE

Edited by ANGIE MANFREDI

Amulet Books · New York

Library of Congress Cataloging-in-Publication Data
Names: Manfredi, Angie, editor.
Title: The (other) F word : a celebration of the fat & fierce /
edited by Angie Manfredi.
Description: New York: Amulet Books, 2019.
Identifiers: LCCN 2019011713 | ISBN 9781419737503 (hardback)
Subjects: LCSH: Body image. | Self-confidence.
Classification: LCC BF697.5.B63 O84 2019 | DDC 306.4/613—dc23

For author and illustrator copyrights, see page 216.
Illustrations copyright © 2019 Lisa Tegtmeier
Book design by Hana Anouk Nakamura

This book was set using: Grotto Sarcasm, by Matteo Bologna © Muccatypo;
Domaine Text, by Kris Sowersby © the Klim Type Foundry; ZnikomitNo24
by gluk; Poster Bodoni BT © Bitstream; and Eloquent JF Pro by Jason Anthony
Walcott © Jukebox Collection.

Printed and bound in U.S.A.
10 9 8 7 6 5 4 3 2 1

Amulet Books are available at special discounts when purchased in quantity for
premiums and promotions as well as fundraising or educational use. Special
editions can also be created to specification. For details, contact
specialsales@abramsbooks.com or the address below.

Amulet Books® is a registered trademark of Harry N. Abrams, Inc.

ABRAMS The Art of Books
195 Broadway, New York, NY 10007
abramsbooks.com

For my parents, Roy and Mary Alice Manfredi, who taught me to take this world on with fearless confidence. And for every fat teenager reading this: there's so much greatness out here waiting for you. Come find us, we love you.

CONTENTS

Dear Reader,

Your body is perfect. Yes, yours. Exactly the way it is, right now in this second.

That's the first thing I want everyone who picks up this book to know. But especially all the fat readers. This book is a love letter to you and a guidebook on how to navigate this world . . . and maybe even a blueprint for how to change it.

There are so many moments in your life as a fat person that are burned into your brain: the first time you awkwardly pulled down a shirt to cover yourself up on the beach when everyone else was pulling clothes off, the first time you heard a skinny friend call themselves FAT like it was the worst thing they could possibly be, the first time you went into a store and realized that even their "plus"-size section didn't have anything that would fit you, the first time someone who cared about you said something about how much prettier/more handsome you would look if you were just a few pounds lighter. Now imagine you've had all those experiences—and more—before you even turn eighteen. Many of you have lived that and much worse. And many of you are living through hard times right now. And I want you to know that so many people understand how it can be so hard and so lonely.

But there's another moment more and more fat people are getting to experience: the first moment they realize there's nothing wrong with being fat.

The book you are holding in your hands is about all those moments and, moreover, it's about helping you get to that second moment. I have always believed that when we learn to accept our bodies the way they are—when we learn to love ourselves exactly as we are in the immediate moment—it can shift the world. And now, with this book, with these words, I hope that YOU can begin to change your world and in doing that maybe change a little bit of the rest of the world too.

When I assembled the 30 voices in this anthology, I strove to portray the entire fullness of the fat experience. So often when you hear people talk about "body positivity" you see able-bodied, white women who are a size 12. I wanted this anthology to move past this small box, and so, within these pages, you'll hear from queer fat people, disabled fat people, and fat IPOC (Indigenous/people of color). There are voices in this book of superfat runway models and fat poets, artists, entrepreneurs, designers, writers, and scholars. This is a book that encompasses the true breadth and depth of fat life in a unique way that I think will give you a chance to see all the possibilities of living a full, happy, fun life as a fat person. You can have all this, and more, and all your dreams can come true. None of it depends on what size pants you wear.

More than anything, this is a book about love. If I had to come back to the one theme that brought all these pieces together, it's how much love they were all written with. It's a note, from the other side, from all the fat people who have had that other moment: the moment when they know that hating yourself is a losing game, the moment when they know it's OK to wear the crop top, the moment they stop apologizing and start living. We love you, and we want you to know that you're not alone. There's a whole community of fat people waiting for you, and we think you're awesome. We made you this book because we want you to know that you're important and you matter. Thank you for reading this book, for sharing it, for helping spread the moments that can change the world.

Your body is perfect. Yes, yours. Exactly the way it is, right now in this second.

Don't ever forget it,

Angie Manfredi

ANGIE MANFREDI

is a librarian and writer who owns every season of *Law & Order* on DVD and sends over 150 handwritten valentines every year. She is a passionate advocate for literacy, diversity, and decolonizing the discourse surrounding children's literature. Angie enjoys watching obscure world cinema, traveling, and trying out regional sodas, and must insist there's no way Jack could've fit on that door in the freezing cold ocean. You can find her writing in the YA anthology *Here We Are: Feminism for the Real World* and online at www.fatgirlreading.com and on Twitter @misskubelik.

Body Sovereignty: This Fat Trans Flesh Is Mine

by
ALEX GINO

I live at the crossroads of fat and trans. I have navigated this body through a web of medical professionals (and unprofessionals) and a society that tries to tell me how my body should be. I'm bombarded with advertisements from a diet industry that wants me to literally be less, along with media that believes that my fat is a moral failing. I've also had to jump through hoops and bear substandard medical care in order to ensure my access to hormones.

On the one hand, my people and I say, "I don't need to change my body," while on the other, we say, "I have every right to." This does not mean that fat and trans communities are at odds. Nor that fat people can't lose weight or that trans people need to medically transition. It comes down to choice. Honest choice. And that comes down to body sovereignty.

Body sovereignty is the belief in self-determination of our own skins and everything inside them. Body sovereignty says this fat trans flesh is mine, and I get to choose what happens to it. Me. For my well-being as I know it to be.

Here's a little chart I made:

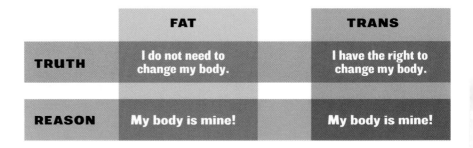

	FAT	TRANS
TRUTH	I do not need to change my body.	I have the right to change my body.
REASON	My body is mine!	My body is mine!

I am *highly* skeptical of the ease with which many doctors recommend radical diets and weight-loss surgeries. I am also *highly* skeptical of barriers to gender-affirming hormones and surgeries. In case that sounds like something doesn't line up, I want to bust open a nugget that will help bring nuance to the matter: purpose. Why does a person want to be smaller? Why does a person want to transition, whatever that change looks like for them?

The fat person who becomes thin is a cultural hero. They have defeated the demons of fat and sugar and sloth and receive accolades of moral triumph. Even if that change is at the expense of their health. Even if that change is a result of illness itself. But the trans person who transitions is a burden. There are new names and pronouns to learn, mistakes not to make. Public questions of bathrooms and athletic competitions. We complicate the system by making the system visible. The norm only exists if there is an abnormal to compare it to.

While a fat person losing weight is often seen as the birth of a "whole new you," transitioning is often seen as a death. There's a common fear, especially among families, of "losing" someone if we transition. A family member once told me not to ask her to use my name because it made her feel like "birth name" was dead. No, really. She has come around since then and uses my name and pronouns. Hurray for growth, but it doesn't change that her comment hurt me and our relationship.

And that's not to mention dating and sex! Many fat people try to change their bodies for their partners, or potential partners. Many trans people fear losing partners, or potential partners, if they come out or transition. The good news for trans folk is that many couples do stay together, and grow closer, once both partners are able to share more of themselves. It's not always immediate, and there are good and bad moments, but there's so much more potential for emotional intimacy when you're able to bring your full self to the table.

The same thing is true for fat folk. Partners who want you to diet so that you will be more attractive to them are scum. And even the ones worried about your health are caught up in a modern myth. The idea that "thin is healthy" is a lie. Losing large amounts of weight, only to gain back more, is a natural effect of dieting, as the body learns that starvation mode is around every corner and builds its defenses. Health is something we control a lot less than the diet industry would like us to believe. It is tied up in our genes, our histories, our resources, and our communities, and none of it is about morality.

Medical intervention is jammed down fat peoples' throats, rather literally in the case of feeding tube diets, which is a real thing that doctors prescribe. Feeding tubes are a valuable tool for people who benefit from them; but wanting to be thinner is a questionable motivator, and feeding tubes do not support someone in developing a better relationship with solid food. But nothing is too risky or untested to try in the name of "weight control."

In contrast, many trans people are denied medical intervention unless and until we perform to a doctor's standard. And even then, we are monitored heavily. I take hormones, and my blood levels are tested regularly, often twice a year, for my "safety." All's well and fine while the numbers look good, but the moment that my physical health competes with my emotional health, medical experts may well make the decision for me and refuse to prescribe my hormones.

Dueling medicalizations create a special dance when trans people are denied surgery unless they lose weight. I can't count how many transmasculine folk I have witnessed lament that they can't get top surgery until they drop an arbitrary number of pounds. And most of them are right that doctors won't operate on them, but they say it with a note of shame instead of indignation, as though they are not worthy of surgery until they are less fat. As if it isn't ridiculous that they aren't allowed to change their bodies for themselves until they change their bodies for a doctor. As if it's reasonable for doctors to use excuses like "the results don't look as good on larger bodies" instead of learning how to operate on us.

The fat body that loses weight is conforming, where the trans body that takes hormones and/or has surgery (or surgeries) is pushing against conformity for the right to exist. And there's another difference: Weight loss is generally temporary and takes work and sacrifice to maintain.

Transition, whether social, medical, or both, allows people to flourish. Diets don't work. Transition does.

The idea that "thin is healthy" is a lie.

As fat and trans people, our body sovereignties are questioned on a daily basis. We are ridiculed and our bodies are turned into jokes. This dehumanization puts us at risk, not only in bearing the emotional brunt of society's scorn, but for physical violence. There is a balance between safety and connection, and sometimes we need to juggle between sharing ourselves and keeping ourselves hidden and safe to share another day. Please, in your quest for body sovereignty, consider your safety a valuable piece of the equation. And if you see someone else being harassed for celebrating their body sovereignty, consider whether it's safe for you to say hi to them, and ask if they'd like you to stick around.

But even when it's questioned, we have the right to body sovereignty. Even when that right is delayed or withheld. Even when we withhold it from ourselves. You get to change your body, even if that complicates someone else's plan. And if changing your body is someone else's plan, you don't have to participate. Either way, it is your right to determine for yourself what happens to your body. And if someone is stopping you from doing that, they are violating your right to body sovereignty.

What can body sovereignty look like? Well, all sorts of things:

- Eating in public
- Eating candy in public
- Eating candy in the park at 10 a.m. while smiling at people taking their daily run
- Running in the park at 10 a.m. while smiling at people eating candy
- Shaving your body
- Not shaving your body
- Shaving half your body
- Shaving your head
- Not cutting or processing your hair
- Wearing that bright yellow dress
- Wearing that bright yellow bikini
- Wearing nothing at all
- Taking off your bra in the car after work
- Not wearing a bra in the first place
- Taking off your prosthetic limb when you get itchy
- Wearing lipstick that complements your mustache
- Tossing out magazines that tell you your body is wrong
- Choosing media that celebrate people like you
- Ordering dessert and eating every last bite
- Reading this book with the cover displayed wide

Body sovereignty is doing something because you want to, not because you're supposed to. A fat man eating ice cream in public is an act of protest against a world that shames and demonizes him. A tall trans woman who wears six-inch heels flaunts her pride in the face of gender norms. A Black nonbinary person who wears their kinky hair naturally looks white beauty standards in the eye and says, "I don't need you."

I was nineteen before I found the word *genderqueer* in *Gender Outlaw: On Men, Women, and the Rest of Us* by Kate Bornstein and quickly took it on. (Thank you forever, Auntie Kate, for letting me know that I am real and that there is a *rest of us*.) And while it was deep in my head, I didn't actually say the word *fat* until I was twenty-three, when reading *Fat!So?* by Marilyn Wann out loud with my dear friend Beth. I was an adult before I was able to describe my body, and both times, it was a book that got me there.

So yeah, that's me ending with a shameless plug to read. The better informed you are, the more the decisions you make are genuinely yours. But no matter where you get your information, study it. Question it. Does it match what you know about yourself? Does it bring in new ideas worth exploring? Or is it trying to get you to follow it instead of yourself? You can tell it to stop.

Remember, you have body sovereignty.

ALEX GINO

loves glitter, ice cream, gardening, awe-ful puns, and stories that reflect the diversity and complexity of being alive. They would take a coffee date with a good friend over a big party any day. Alex is the author of middle-grade novels *You Don't Know Everything, Jilly P!* and the Stonewall Award–winning *George.* You can read more about their books and thoughts at alexgino.com and on Twitter @lxgino.

Chubby
City
Indian

by
JANA SCHMIEDING

When I was growing up, I felt like I was living two different lives on two opposite riverbanks. On one riverbank was my existence at school in a small town in Oregon. This reality was dominated by whiteness, and the narratives of "others" were taught incorrectly in history textbooks through harrowing stories of westward expansion. Over there, I struggled daily to remain small and friendly in order to avoid being publicly shamed by powerful white girls. I wrote dry reports about Lewis and Clark's bravery along with my peers, conveniently leaving out the part of the story where an enslaved Shoshone teen was sent on their mission with them, carrying a baby across treacherous terrain, as a guide and translator for two white heroes.

Swimming to the other side of the bank—through a swiftly moving current of time and progress—was worth it; for on the other side of the river, I was Indigenous. My mother's family are of the Lakota Sioux Tribe and my siblings and I were raised as traditional dancers and members of a tightly knit intertribal community. In these Indigenous spaces, womanhood was honored, and beauty was readily found in one's commitment to keeping the community sacred and healthy. Children were raised to cherish our elderly and to adore the process of aging. Adults were concerned less with status and more with ensuring that their children maintained a touchstone to our Indigenous identity—a selfhood that had been taken from us and systematically erased since the arrival of Columbus.

Only now—as a grown woman who has lived many lives in many different bodies—have I allowed the river of time and progress to flood, making these banks insignificant. Now I take joy in swimming in my life's muddy water, caring less and less about what my swimwear looks like atop my rolling curves. Instead, I let life's swift currents brush against my vulnerable, exposed skin. I find solace in knowing that if I were to go under, I could navigate choppy conditions. Both sides of the river provide a gentle incline for me to step on in order to get my bearings, so that I might belly flop back into a steady stroke against life's tumultuous stream.

THE WHITE SIDE OF THE RIVER

Middle school in the nineties was absolutely brutal for a young woman with already large breasts and thighs.

In ye old days before Instagram, people weren't bombarded twenty-four seven with thin influencers and "body positive yoga warriors" against which we could compare ourselves. We used what was available to us. We pitted our bodies against women in pop music and movies, women on television, and of course, women within the vicious, thin hierarchy of our peers. I was good at comparing my body to all the above. I've never received an athletic award or trophy despite a sporty youth. I've never triumphed in the talent show over all my classmates despite having a lovely voice (if I may brag). But I could have won first place in comparing my body to other women: That's where my true genius resided.

This place, this untamed frontier of heartbreak, this Wild West of adolescent abandon, this place called SCHOOL, was where we as young women learned how to see ourselves. We learned with each other how cigarettes felt to smoke and how brave we were when squaring off with another angry girl. And then there were boys. We learned about the intentions of boys in middle school, because they had somewhat caught up with us. Movies and television taught us how to decode their behaviors, and we aimed to please.

It was important to know how they felt about us—where we stood with the boys—because we based our every decision on their anticipated responses. This was our first true encounter with the *male gaze*. Our entire world was (and is) curated, seen, and evaluated by men. We women are objects on their world's stage—malleable figures open to scrutiny of the male lens.

I once watched a group of girls dump a carton of cottage cheese all over the outside of a classmate named Coleen's locker. When she arrived at her locker, she was the laughingstock of the hallway. Kids yelled, "Cottage cheese! Cottage cheese!" in reference to the cellulite on her thighs that was visible when she wore short shorts, which she often proudly did. This was an act of retaliation by a group of girls who had been brainwashed to see themselves through the telescope-like lens of the male gaze. They had learned that cellulite, or really any kind of fat on a woman's body, was incorrect and therefore a fair target. And the cellulite was simply a focus for their hatred. What they were truly threatened by was Coleen's unwavering sexuality. They were slut-shaming her with dairy products. While the hallway roared with laughter, every girl present—myself included—carefully folded her arms across her body and prayed a silent prayer to herself that no one would ever see the rolls under her T-shirt or the dimples that were developing across her butt cheeks.

I came into middle school with a plan. By then I had a jiggly stomach—one that would never even *pretend* to form a six-pack no matter how little food I ate or how many sit-ups I did—and I knew right away that I wasn't going to deliver the kind of femininity boys required. I was constantly subconsciously preventing another cottage cheese incident.

Whatever the case, my brilliant plan to bring boys—these instant kings—into my orbit was by befriending them. I was damn good at it, too! I would let boys cheat off my homework and belch in my face. They loved pushing me into the swimming pool and throwing snacks down my cleavage like it was a basketball hoop. It was cool! I was fine with it! Whatever! We got along fantastically as friends, and I relished the attention I got from my attractive "buds." We were thick as thieves, and I lived for their affection. I knew that I didn't want to get too close to the center of their telescope lenses, because my boobs were growing by the day and my cheeks were filling out. Who knows what ridicule would befall me if I allowed the male gaze to see me as . . . *gulp* . . . sexy?

I was afraid of anything sexual. I'd had a couple of boyfriends, but I remember breaking up with one of them after a week of feeling really uncomfortable with the way he was parading me around as his "girlfriend"—like a trophy. When I told him I just wanted to be friends, he did not handle it graciously. He announced to anyone who might be listening, "Hey, Jana has zits on her arms!" I had a skin condition called keratosis pilaris that caused the pores on my arms to clog and rise, and

I often scratched the bumps or picked at them. After my ex-boyfriend's pronouncement, I stopped wearing tank tops. From then on, I resolved, no boy would see my arms. I had been exposed once, and I wouldn't let it happen again.

The pressure from my adolescent peers to exhibit public displays of affection was beginning to mount. "Kiss him! Use your tongue!" they would call out if a two-week flame and I were sitting together at lunch. All the while, I desperately wanted a boy to desire me for my winning personality instead of my increasingly cumbersome breasts. Now that maturity was requiring me to wear two sports bras for basketball games, I also began to sense if a dude was more interested in the bigness of my boobs than the timing of my jokes. School was an increasingly dangerous place. There were decisions we made there about our bodies that would scar us for a lifetime. We were starving ourselves to fit into a narrow lens, and even if we managed to fit, our whole selves often went unseen. So I maintained a sort of neutral invisibility. As my body grew more curvaceous, I managed its exposure by pleasing others with kindness and friendship and hiding the prouder, more passionate parts of me so they wouldn't get mocked in the hallway like Coleen.

THE NATIVE SIDE OF THE RIVER

I began dancing in powwows when I was old enough to walk. As I grew up, one of the few Natives in a predominantly white community, I came to understand powwows as a crucial element to our Indigenous survival.

I attended powwows with my grandparents, parents, and siblings. They took place in high school gymnasiums when the Northwest rain was a looming inevitability and on fairgrounds or in fields in the dry months of late summer. I relished the day-long, sometimes weekend-long, activities involved in powwowing. The smell of the steaming iron against the fabric of our ribbon dresses; lacing the soft leather moccasins snugly around my feet and legs; the alarming whiplash of my neck as my hair got yanked back into two tight braids. Powwows are a gathering for Native folks from all different paths. It is where we can put aside our traumas from a genocidal history and thrive in a space of self-expression and joy.

Traditional dancing came naturally to me. The sound of the drum and breathtaking falsetto of the men and women singing our songs while we danced in a great circle was rooted in something ancient and precious. It felt as if something lost was being recovered and celebrated; and indeed, it was. Around the age of eight or nine, I started to get serious about being a fancy shawl dancer. Many of the older girls that I would powwow with, including my older sister, were already bounding across the floor under colorful, fringed shawls, their feet improvising elaborate steps, kicks, and turns that matched the swift rhythm of the drum.

There was an incredible unspoken kinship with other Native young women, women who were also going to a place called school during the week, who were also learning about Native Americans from textbooks in social studies classes and having to dress up as pilgrims for kindergarten pageants. I compared myself to them but not in the same way that I measured my bulbous body against the thin and angular white girls at school. This was a different kind of comparison that involved watching, learning, and honoring the skillful womanhood that my older peers were displaying.

It was safe and normal in the Native community to see myself as complex: both as an individual and as an important part of a group of other women, because we looked to each other as teachers, not competition. We relied on each other to uphold this invaluable space for ourselves, our community, our ancestors, and those who were not yet born.

I got to watch women of all shapes and sizes dance traditionally, and there were so many different iterations and styles of dancing at a powwow. Even when dancing competitively, one could not help but celebrate our presence—our permanence—despite the wicked genocide our people had experienced at the hands of colonization, and the resulting alienation we've endured. When our intertribal

I got to watch women of all shapes and sizes dance.

communities came together, we did not scrutinize the amount of space our bodies took up. In fact, if you were to see the grandness of the dancing at a powwow or the elaborate regalia of a fancy shawl dancer, or the strength and nobility of a Women's Traditional dancer under the heaviness of her floor-length buckskin dress, you would observe that the objective is to respectfully and beautifully utilize space—all of it. It was wonderful that our varied bodies were there together, moving to our music, expressing ourselves in our own ways no matter our shape or size. Elderly people and toddlers alike with thick and strong bodies took themselves to the center of the dance floor with feathered fans held proudly in the air. Women with larger breasts and hips bounded nimbly across the floor to brandish their brilliant shawls and delight us with the rhythmic shuffling of their jingle dresses.

These were my two worlds—my two riverbanks. On one side of the river, my value came solely from my body in contrast to others' and its passing or failing of the male inspection. It was a messy, failed body before it even knew itself, and for that reason, I was hopeless more often than hopeful in this world. I was always striving to climb some invisible pyramid of beauty, money, thinness, and whiteness.

But on certain occasions and especially in the summertime, I was relieved to cross my life's river to the side where I was Indigenous. On that side I was a woman complete: full of laughter and hope. More important, I was a keeper of something meaningful. My womanhood was honored, and no matter my body's size or degree of fatness, it was seen as sacred— a vessel for our people's history and our future. Dancing traditionally was my way of honoring the other women in my life. My bigness and boldness on the dance floor were a celebration of their courage and endurance in the face of so much historic silencing. I was a dancer, and when I danced, I did so with generations of ancestors at my wings.

ARI SCOTT

JANA SCHMIEDING

is a Lakota Native writer, producer, educator, and activist working to move the needle of representation in media and entertainment toward including the fascinating stories of Native women. She hosts and produces a podcast called *Woman of Size* on the WhoHaha Podcast Network that explores feminist narratives of people with marginalized bodies, and her current screenwriting projects all feature Native female protagonists. You can follow her podcast at womanof size.com or on Twitter and Instagram @womanofsizepod.

How to Be the Star of Your Own Fat Rom-Com

by
LILY ANDERSON

Romantic comedies can start anywhere—a classroom, a bookstore, the middle of the street. Whether you're a sweet cinnamon roll, a raunchy bro, or the overall-clad artist just waiting to be made over for prom: Your romance is out there, waiting for you, Fat Babe.

STEP 1. BE THE BEST HERO YOU CAN BE

A good romantic comedy lead is the one who is being authentically themselves. You're living your life out loud, not waiting around for life to happen to you. You're doing stuff you love (hanging with friends, crushing your extracurriculars, reading dope books like this one).

You're not waiting for love. You're cultivating a totally you, totally full life where love is welcome to walk in the door at any moment. Because YOU are a complete person already. You're not looking for another half, Fat Babe. You're looking for someone worthy of all that love you have to give.

Being authentically you doesn't mean refusing to change or digging your heels in when choices aren't working. You're a biological organism— sometimes, you gotta grow! Just because you've never done something (like public speaking or skydiving), doesn't mean you never will. Keep your heart open and your eyes clear!

Avoid This Trope: Don't Sidekick Yourself

G rowing up, we all see and hear a lot of fatphobia that can make us feel like we'll never be the star of our own lives. In movies and on TV, fat folks are often the sidekicks and that can make us feel like that's our only role to play in life. You might feel like your fatness somehow makes you less deserving of attention.

No way! Don't you dare put yourself on the sidelines, Fat Babe! You are just as worthy of the spotlight as anyone else. You weren't born to let other people shine for you. Your story has already started, and you've been the star the whole time. Act like it!

STEP 2. LOCK DOWN YOUR LOOK

L et me tell you, as someone who has seen plastic chokers come back into fashion twice (?!), wear whatever makes you feel hot. As a teen-ager, I wore Frederick's of Hollywood corsets as tops, dyed my hair orange, and once had a giant Claire's snake necklace that I wore for three years *in a row* because it made me feel like a fat Joan Jett. Was I? I don't know. Did Joan Jett have a skirt made from a *Fiddler on the Roof* souvenir T-shirt? Probably not!

Chase *your* fashion bliss. Get down with your fat self. Thrift stores, resale websites, and the clearance racks at department stores are here for you. Don't be afraid to make alterations or additions where you see fit. Shop in both the men's and women's sections, because gendered clothing is arbitrary!

Avoid This Trope: The "Flattering" Wardrobe

"Flattering" is trash. It means that the clothes are actively hiding something that society has deemed not good enough. Don't go hiding your arms because of what someone else might think of them. Those are *your* arms. They carry your hopes and dreams and heavy books and deserve to see the sun.

If you want to rock out with your tum out, do it. If you want the world to see your rolls, go for it. This is the only body you get, and it should be your friend. Dress it up however you want. Fuck the rules. You will look your best when you *feel* like you look your best. You're never fully dressed without a positive attitude about your outfit.

STEP 3. GET YOUR ENSEMBLE CAST READY

Make sure you have a good sounding board. You can't do it all on your own, every day. Sometimes you will need other points of view to help you find your way through a situation.

Who are your go-to friends? Do you already have a sassy sidekick who will push you out of your comfort zone? A crew of like-minded weirdos who always have your back?

Whether you're developing new friendships or surrounded by your lifelong pals, make sure you have some cool platonic folks around. Siblings, cousins, and quirky grandparents may also apply. The Internet can be great for this, too! Long-distance friends and message-board compatriots are totally valid. Some of my best friends in the world I met on Twitter!

Avoid This Trope: The Frenemies

Life is too short to hang with people who make you feel bad. People who demand favors but never show up for you. People who make "jokes" that are really insults. People who use the word *fat* as an insult or harmful self-deprecation—"*I feel so fat today!*"

Well, la-di-dah, Hypothetical Fatphobe Friend, because I'm fat every day, and I feel great.

If someone in your life is making you feel small or stupid, speak up for yourself, Fat Babe, and then walk away. Be clear about your feelings *in the moment* to save yourself from being miserable in the future. Advocate for yourself the way you would advocate for someone you love—because *no one* is more deserving of your love than you are. You wouldn't let your friends slander each other or themselves. Don't you dare let them do it to you. If someone says something hurtful, respond with, "That hurt my feelings," or, "Please don't talk about me that way." And if they are unwilling to work with you, they're probably not a good friend.

STEP 4. FINDING YOUR LOVE INTEREST

This is the hard part. Finding the perfect love interest for you is definitely a question of personal taste. Is it your long-standing crush? The class clown in the back of the room? Your nemesis? (Everyone loves an enemies-to-lovers story!) Find someone who makes your heart sing and your palms sweat in that way that makes you feel like the shiniest star in the sky. Because you are! Did you know that no one else in the whole world has ever been or ever will be you? OMG, Fat Babe! You're basically the rarest gem. No wonder you're the lead of this rom-com.

Avoid This Trope: Secret Relationships

Watch out for people who make you feel *almost* shiny enough. You don't deserve to be anyone's secret sweetheart or sidepiece. Your fat body isn't something for someone else to "get over" or to "like you in spite of." There are people in the world who will be attracted to you the way you are right now, without any caveats. Those people deserve to costar in your romantic comedy. Not people who won't let you meet their friends or don't put pictures of you on social media.

STEP 5. THE MEET-CUTE

OK, so you can't *exactly* plot this one out. A "meet-cute" is that moment in the rom-com when the two love interests are in the same place at the same time for the first time. The inciting incident.

Spontaneity is the hallmark of a meet-cute. However, there's no rule against putting yourself in places where the meet cute is more likely to happen. For instance:

- the cafeteria
- a street fair
- comic book stores
- message boards
- the library
- coffee shops
- group hangs (also known by their much scarier title, *parties*)

Avoid This Trope: Pretending to Be Someone You're Not

Lying is not the way into anyone's heart. Besides being rude, it sets you on a road that can only end in failure. When the lie comes out, no matter how well intentioned, the person who was lied to has every right to walk away from you. Being earnest is usually an equally easy way in and rarely blows up in your face.

So, instead of pretending to be a marine biologist, try: "I know you're a marine biologist. I'd love to know more about that."

Instead of pretending to like baseball, try: "I get the base system, but what do people in the field even do?"

Instead of pretending to be someone without depression, try: "I have clinical depression, so I'm not as energetic as usual today."

It's harder to pretend to be someone else than it is to be great at being you. Who wants to be a mediocre copy when you could be a limited edition? Your authentic self is what draws people to you. Practice loving things unabashedly—whether it's the media you consume, the topics you geek out about, or the fat body you live in. Confidence begets more confidence.

STEP 6. WE SHOULD HANG OUT

It's the falling-in-love montage! Love is the roots of friendship blooming into a new plant. So this step is about getting your friendship seeds planted.

When you feel comfortable and safe, it's time for you and your love interest to be alone together. You're actively making memories together and discovering your differences. You're comparing biographies, seeing which of your ideas fit together. Make sure you're with someone who is as interested in why you're you as they are in telling you why they're them. You're more than just a reflective surface for them to see themselves in.

Avoid This Trope: You're My Whole Life Now

It's fun to have fun, but you need downtime. Remember your ensemble cast? They're still worthy of spending time with you, even if they aren't in the middle of their own whirlwind romance. Keep up your normal life. See your friends, pet your cat, and maintain your hobbies. All the spheres of your life deserve to engage with you when you're happy, not just one person. No one appreciates being forgotten when their friend falls in love, only to be remembered when that friend suddenly needs help.

You're learning to balance, so sometimes you'll fall over. But learn from the fall.

STEP 7. CONSENT IS SEXY

Not everyone is into sexual activity (Hey, ace friends!), and not everyone is ready for sexy times, but if you are, cool! This step is for you.

We're all used to that big movie kiss (you know the one, where their mouths don't seem to quite meet up, but the music is swelling so loudly you don't notice). But movies are terrible at showing us consent. Kissing people who aren't expecting it isn't swoony, it's rape-y. Normalize your own use of "May I" or "I would like" in sexual and physical situations, so that you aren't progressing without establishing consent. With a partner you trust, you can find your nonverbal cues or safe words. Being safe means being communicative.

Also, be courteous of the world around you. Your sex life is a private thing—not because it's shameful or wrong, but because only the people involved consented to it. Don't shove it under anyone's nose.

Avoid This Trope: Too Much Too Soon

No one needs the exact same amount of sexual contact every day. So sometimes, you're going to find a day when maybe you just don't wanna. Maybe it's the first time you try to make out after eating a whole burrito (bad idea). Maybe it's the millionth time you've been with someone, but this time doesn't feel right. Maybe you were triggered by something sensory and you need a pause while you regain your equilibrium.

You are *always, always, always* entitled to stop any sexual interaction. You are allowed to say no after you've said yes. Your partner might be startled or even upset, but be as clear about your reasons as you can be and firm in your resolve. Even if they threaten you or gaslight you with bullshit ideas like "no one else will want you." I promise, there will be more than one person who finds you sexually desirable. It's a big giant world and you've got a big giant heart. There will be scores of people who want to costar in your story. The most important thing is that you find someone safe and trustworthy.

Here are some examples of how you can be clear about what you want and need:

- "You did nothing wrong, but I need a moment."
- "I did not like what was happening, so I need this to be over."
- "I am so queasy right now. Why did we eat giant burritos first?"

Regardless of the *why*, you get to stop when needed. And your partner gets to stop as needed. This is not up for debate.

STEP 8. THE BIG FIGHT

Sorry, Fat Babe, but the big fight comes to every relationship someday. The same way you disagree with your besties, siblings, and sometimes the person ahead of you in traffic. You and your love interest are different people with different points of view. So someday you are going to have a disagreement that feels like an earthquake. Maybe it's a careless word choice or a huge oversight. Either way, you'll need to retreat to your separate support systems (in split screen and one side is probably playing a game of pickup basketball while discussing the issue).

Presuppose the best of your partner, and understand that few people work out of purely malicious intent (but some people certainly do). Be clear about what your heart needs to heal, whether it's an apology or acknowledgment of your feelings. No one reads minds. People need to learn before they can know.

Avoid This Trope: Throwing It All Away for Pride

Don't throw away a relationship rather than compromise. Everyone has deal breakers (like racism, fatphobia, and other hate speech), but be aware when you're being petulant or arbitrary. Just because you don't adore their favorite restaurant doesn't mean you can't eat there on occasion. If you want people to respect things that are special to you, sometimes you have to respect things that are special to them.

STEP 9. HAPPILY EVER WORKING ON IT

There's no timeline for relationship milestones, no matter what people try to tell you. You will see people who say "I love you" on the first date and stay married for fifty years. You will see people move in together too soon, too late, or never. You will hear about relationship dynamics that make no sense to you at all.

The only people in your relationship are you and your partner(s). Your relationship will become a quilt of the experiences and expectations you share. Find your mission statement, and let your partner in on it. "I want to find happiness in the small things." "I want to experience every part of the world." "I want to be a strong member of my community." Work toward a common goal together, even if that goal is deeper happiness.

Avoid This Trope: The Curated Couple

Beware becoming the couple who does everything perfectly, especially through the lens of a camera. If all your privacy is public, what's left to be special? Social media may have its milestone moments (you know them: the black-and-white holding-hands shot, the public-kiss selfie, the pretending to be asleep even though someone had to take the picture), but it's not real life. Your relationship isn't a scavenger hunt of clichés. There is so much more to life than clichés. Just like learning to embrace and celebrate your fat body exactly as it is, you can celebrate your relationship sincerely, not the way you think it's supposed to look. Real milestone moments in relationships—and in life—are the ones that *we* create, not the ones created for us.

EPILOGUE. **WHEN THE ROM GOES OUT OF YOUR COM**

Breakups happen, dear hearts. Not everyone gets to lock down their perfect someone on the first (or tenth) try. Be kind to yourself, load up on self-care gear (books, face masks, snacks, music to wallow to), and remember: Tomorrow could be the day your next meet-cute hits. Be ready, Fat Babe.

And remember: You're the star.

LILY ANDERSON

is the author of *The Only Thing Worse Than Me Is You*, *Not Now Not Ever*, and *Undead Girl Gang*. A former school librarian, she is deeply devoted to Shakespeare, fairy tales, and podcasts. Somewhere in Northern California, she is having strong opinions on musical theater. Find her online at mslilyanderson.com

The Story of My Body

by
RENÉE WATSON

And when I say fat it is not insult or disclaimer.
My body does not apologize for being big, for being Black,
for being woman.

And when I say my body, what I mean is my belly. Round
and full of my momma's home cooking: smoked neckbones,
collards, curry goat, fried fish. How my belly aches from
dinner-table laughter, how it aches with cramps once a month,
reminding me how woman I am.

These hands that have held handfuls of my niece's thick hair.
Held it and braided it and made calm out of chaos. These
hands that have cradled nephews, that have folded in prayer.
Hands that clung to my big sister when we walked home from
the park. Hands that still want to reach out for her, even
though now I am too old. Hands that fidget and twist when
people say, "You have a cute face." Ignoring the rest of my body.

And when I say my body, what I mean is my hair that has a story all its own. How it morphs into curls and waves and crinkles. How it disguises itself in braids and twists.

I mean my legs and feet that have taken me to the edge of the beach, Pacific Ocean at the tip of my toes. I mean these eyes. Brown like my daddy's. These eyes that have seen the miracle of sunsets and moonlight, the majesty of mountain and waterfall.

I mean these eyes that wept for Trayvon, Michael, Eric, Renisha, Sandra. Wept when my momma's doctor told us she had cancer. Wept when Grandpa died.

Wept when that man touched me and told me he knew what to do to big girls like me, knew how to handle my body. And when I pushed his hands off my body, I was pushing him off my skin that has a scar, a scar from the time my knee split open after a fall off my Strawberry Shortcake bike, my skin that gushed out a river of blood onto dirt and pebbles, my skin that stung when the Band-Aid was ripped off. My scarred skin, first rough, then smooth.

A reminder that my body heals.

This is what I mean.
These parts, these stories.
All housed in this fat, Black, girl body.

These stories, these parts.
All me.

RENÉE WATSON

is the *New York Times* bestselling author of *Piecing Me Together*, which received a Coretta Scott King Award and Newbery Honor. Her writing often centers around the experiences of Black girls and women and explores themes of home, identity, and the intersections of race, class, and gender. Renée is the founder of the I, Too Arts Collective, which is housed in the Harlem brownstone where Langston Hughes lived. Renée grew up in Portland, Oregon and currently lives in New York City.

✦∗✦⸫ brighter ✦ than starlight ⸳*✦⸴ ✦

Brighter Than Starlight

(an illustration)

by
JIJI KNIGHT

I used to set *thin* on a pedestal and tell myself, "This is your goal." I wanted to *feel* for once—to *know*—what that confidence tasted like. But when I started to draw myself in my characters and people reached out, I found something so much more valuable. I found happiness. Support. Love. And I found that all of it is simply something I can't measure on a scale. I'll continue to draw fat people, because I want to be a light that reaches back out in the dark for someone who needs it. I want to be that reminder out there that tells you you're beautiful as you are and means it.

JIJI KNIGHT

is a lover of magic, naps, ladies, and breakfast for dinner.
Graphic designer by day and illustrator by night, she's a
champion of body positivity, a uniter of the cute and maca-
bre, and overall dedicates her body of work to women. She
studied illustration at the Academy of Art in beautiful San
Francisco and currently resides in her desert hometown of
Las Vegas. You can find her work online at JijiKnight.com or
on Twitter, Instagram, and other places under @jijidraws.

A Body Like Mine

---

by
MASON DEAVER

Clothing is one of my favorite things to explore. I love experimenting with different looks, styles, patterns, colors. I probably spend far too much time and money in stores and online, looking at things, imagining how I could make them different and create new styles. Recently, I've gotten into altering my own clothing. Dyeing, bleaching, cutting, sewing. It's fun seeing what I can make out of something else.

Even when I'm watching a movie or a television show, my eye is always drawn to what the characters are wearing. No matter if it's a sweet romantic comedy or a sci-fi epic, I'm always interested in the clothing on the screen. I wonder why particular things were chosen and think about how a character's personality or history can be portrayed simply by having good costumes.

Fashion is something I've been interested in for a long time, and as I've gotten older, my passion for it has helped broaden my horizons. It's connected me to my nonbinary identity and helped me feel validated in my choices as I pick outfits from both the male and female sections of stores. I love combining masculine and feminine styles to create a look that I feel represents me.

This love interest of mine is strange, however, because the fashion industry doesn't know what to do with people like me: people who are fat. Being a fat person who loves clothing is a loaded gun. I *love* fashion, and I love clothing. But just as often as my clothing empowers me, it can cause extreme discomfort. Sometimes I can't fit into a certain cute, stylish outfit or a store just doesn't carry *anything* I can wear.

I love clothes, but clothes do not love me back. They don't love the size of my stomach or thighs. It's difficult to describe the experience of being a fat person who loves to go shopping. Sometimes I visit stores early in the morning or late at night to avoid crowds and the judgment of others.

A lot of stores want to make the things that fit me harder to find. They proudly advertise that I can find larger sizes online . . . as though they don't want me shopping there in person. Being nonbinary adds a surreal layer to things, because I don't limit myself to what styles I wear—masculine or feminine. Shopping in a men's section can, at times, be

easy. But often as I move toward the women's sections, plus sizes are tucked into a corner of the store. The message is clear: I'm meant to shop away from the eyes of everyone else.

This experience can be very othering. It doesn't make me feel good knowing that the few people making clothing for fat bodies make them *specifically* for fat bodies, rather than for all different types of people. That instead of mainstream designers offering more sizes, plus-size customers are given a small

corner of the store with limited options while surrounded by other things we can't wear.

My own personal style can only be described as tacky. I love ugly things, especially when they are ugly on purpose. I like loud patterns, colors, hats, and ugly shoes. Still, it took years to cultivate my own style. Despite my being a trans and nonbinary person who loves mixing masculine and feminine fashion, my options were—and sometimes still are—painfully limited.

The beauty of clothing is that it is inherently a genderless form of expression—it has no limits! For trans people, traditionally masculine or feminine clothing can be reaffirming for their gender identity. For fat trans people, there's an extra layer to contend with. It's challenging to find shirts, for example, that aren't revealing of a chest I don't want most people to see. No matter what look I'm going for, I have to be creative in order to hit the style jackpot.

So, then comes the question:

Is there a fix?

I don't have a definitive answer. But there has been movement toward change. Stores are offering more sizes, designers are dressing fat celebrities, fat designers are being given a forum, and as a culture, we're coming to the realization that we shouldn't have to change our physical selves for anyone. (And in the back of this book, you'll find a list of fat fashion references that will, I hope, make things easier for you right now.) In an industry that has profited from designing for skinny bodies, the road to change is one long, complicated puzzle. To push things further, faster, one step we can take is to acknowledge the imbalance. And we can refuse to be ignored. Write letters to your favorite designers! Complain! Walk proudly in the outfits you love. Instagram the shit out of your smiling face when you feel beautiful. We're making slow progress, but we're getting there. And we can get there together—by supporting one another and continuing to speak out. We're here to change the world; why not look amazing while we do it?

MASON DEAVER

is a nonbinary author and bookseller who lives in Charlotte, North Carolina, where the word *y'all* is used in abundance. When they aren't writing or working, they're typically found in their kitchen baking something that's bad for them or out in their garden complaining about the toad that likes to dig holes around their hydrangeas. You can find them online at masondeaverwrites.com and on Twitter @masondeaver.

Fat, And

by
S. QIOUYI LU

0

Take the constant: fat.

What does it mean to be fat? Being fat just means you have one of a range of body types carrying some amount of adipose tissue above an arbitrarily determined average point.

That's it. Being fat doesn't have anything to do with character, health, personality, attractiveness, or worth.

And yet.

1

I'm sure others in this collection will cover the myriad obstacles we face as fat people: the daily struggles, like putting together an inspired outfit from the limited fashion offerings we're afforded. The endless confrontations—whether in doctors' offices or on the street—that divorce our bodies from our humanity. The frustration of never seeing ourselves in fiction or, if we do, seeing ourselves only as the butt of some joke.

So I'll let others tackle that for now.

I want to talk about something else: the way we as people are layered, and never as just one static identity. We cannot be summed up in one term. To examine our multilayered selves, we've got to start with the constant—fat—and set aside the rest.

2

Who is "fat"? When we talk about what it means to be fat, what range of body types are we considering? And above what average point of adipose tissue? But being fat is never really about these abstract numbers or details—

which can and often do change according to age, era, geography, and where you are in your life journey. To illustrate my point, I want to tell my own story.

I don't think it'd be possible to understand my upbringing without understanding the demographics of the area where I grew up. I'm first-generation Chinese American, born in California to two people who emigrated in the eighties from China to the United States to pursue higher education. I grew up in the San Gabriel Valley of Southern California, in a suburb that's half Asian American. By the time I was in high school, most of my classes were predominantly comprised of Asian Americans with a sprinkling of other Indigenous, Black, and/or people of color, and the occasional token white person.

Aside from the demographics and some cultural quirks, my formative years were representative of a fairly typical US upbringing: silly things kids get up to, inexplicable drama, mismatches between parental expectations and kids' agency . . . and, of course, fussing about image.

From a young age—middle school or earlier—both my mother and I berated my thighs for being too large in shorts, my muffin top for spilling over my jeans, my dresses for failing to flatter. I was fortunate enough to travel to China several times growing up. I began to expect that—if I normally wore a medium in the United States—I would be lucky to squeeze into an extra large in China. Most of my friends at the time were other Asian Americans (usually other East Asians), as that was the dominant demographic in my California suburb. It became harder for me to shop with them as my body expanded.

I developed a conscious awareness that I was fat . . . for an Asian person. Even years later as I write this essay, I find the idea nagging me. I'm not fat; I'm only fat . . . for an Asian person.

What does that even mean?

3

Fat . . . *for* an Asian person.

The *for* carries so much weight, despite being such a tiny word.

Let's circle back to that constant: How wide a range of bodies are considered fat? Above what average point of adipose tissue?

For a while, describing myself as "fat for an Asian person" gave me comfort and a clearer sense of self, even as I was learning about fat acceptance. I knew that I had an easier time navigating public spaces and didn't face stigmas as extreme as my larger peers did.

But something felt amiss.

Later, as I developed a stronger racial consciousness and an understanding of Asian oppression, I wondered: What if I were fat . . . *and* Asian?

Fat, *and.*

When I told myself I was fat *for an Asian*, all I could see in fat acceptance communities were people who accepted the constant of *fat* without necessarily examining the added layers. Fat people are more than fat. They can be fat and white, for example. Or fat and Black. Or fat and queer. Sometimes people focus so much on *fat* that they forget to notice the rest.

When fat spaces are defined by a standard of experience created by one dominant group—fat and white, for example—other experiences are quick to be pushed aside. I'm not fat *for* an Asian person; I'm fat *and* Asian. The fact that I am Asian is inextricable from the fact that I am fat. Likewise, the fact that I am fat is inextricable from the fact that I am Asian: The two are deeply intertwined, both socially and medically. When I feel dysphoric about my fat body, my fantasies about my aesthetic ideal are not waifish white women who walk runaways and pose in magazines, but thin Asian women with "watermelon seed faces," as we'd say in Mandarin.

Fat, and.

4

That's the thing with life, with layers, with addition: There's never just one journey going on at a time. In fact, they're all tangled together. You will have to learn to make space for your *and*s.

I'm not sure when I started figuring out that I was nonbinary, or a person whose gender isn't fully male or fully female. The initial few years were filled with so much doubt: Can I be nonbinary if I do this? If I don't do that? If I look this way? If I don't look that way? If I feel this way? If I don't feel that way? Over time, while grappling with reconciling my multiple selves, I've come to realize that the most haunting experiences are the ones where people tell you that your experiences aren't enough or aren't correct.

As I began to seek out resources for nonbinary people, I found photo after photo of people who were assigned female at birth (AFAB) and identified as nonbinary like me. But overwhelmingly, the photos were of thin, white people who were dressed in masculine clothing. I liked my feminine clothing and makeup; I don't think I could ever pass for white even if I tried; and I'd never been thin.

Realizing that all I needed in order to be nonbinary was the knowledge that I *was* nonbinary released me. It allowed me to achieve peace and be loudly and confidently myself. I knew now I didn't have to present a certain way or have a certain body type.

Fat, and . . . nonbinary.

The constant was fat; and there I was again, full circle. The fact that I am nonbinary is inextricable from the fact that I am fat. As with race, when I embraced my identity with the broadening term *and*, I came to understand that expanding spaces to allow for more experiences can only enrich our understanding of ourselves and each other.

What about subtraction?

Being fat is unique as an identity, in that it's physically possible to subtract it. Many identities can be fluid, as with gender; some identities are temporary, but some—like racial identity—are far more fixed.

Imagine the scent of alcohol stinging my nose as I rub a disinfectant wipe on my soft tummy. I am no longer hesitant to jab myself with a needle. "It's an appetite suppressant," the doctor said, "meant to help you lose weight." Since losing weight really is the only way you can treat fatty liver disease—I've done my due diligence—I take my medication.

I still have mixed feelings whenever I look at the injection pen. Am I somehow turning my back on an identity if I lose weight, even if it means I'm healthier in the long run? Isn't that what this is about, health? Or is health just a word people latch on to as a shield to vilify? If all my experiences have been layered on top of each other, like inks mixed together in water, what does it mean if I take one away?

You will have to learn to make space for your *and*s.

Always return to the constants.

When you go through life and learn how to be more resilient, you realize even the supposed constants can wind up changing.

There's a definition for fat; I wrote it up top. But even that shifts. For better or worse, even that changes.

There's a trick to understanding yourself: Identities are not fixed. From race to size to everything in between, these are not templates. They're tools for parsing your own experience. As soon as they don't work, you can set them aside and use something else. You can shelve them for later. Or you pick up one you'd tossed aside, one that wasn't working before but that you need now. You have the right to do that. You have the right to find what works for *you*, to keep looking, to decide for yourself.

So here I am now: fat, *and* Asian, *and* nonbinary. *And* disabled, *and* bisexual, *and* a million other identities, *and* a million other things that are qualities rather than identities. Every single part of me influences the others. In the future if I am no longer fat, that is OK, too. It doesn't erase who I was or what I experienced.

Fat, *and* multitudes.

There's room here for you, too.

S. QIOUYI LU

writes, translates, and interprets between two coasts of the Pacific. Their fiction and poetry have appeared in *Asimov's Science Fiction, The Magazine of Fantasy & Science Fiction*, and *Uncanny*. Their translations have appeared in *Clarkesworld,* and they edit the flash fiction and poetry magazine *Arsenika*. You can find out more about S. at their website, s.qiouyi.lu.

Write Something Fat

by
SARAH HOLLOWELL

Dear Sarah,

You're sixteen and you're participating in your first National Novel Writing Month. You're embarking on a wild adventure—writing a fifty-thousand-word novel in the thirty days of November. You've never written a novel before, but it's all you've wanted to do since you were ten, so here you are. You build a fantasy world full of magic and angels and pirates and brothers turned into rabbits. You imagine a million details to fill out fifty thousand words.

You don't imagine that it's a world accepting of fat people.

Your heroine is small and slim, because that's what heroines are. The beautiful people she meets are slender, because that's what the beautiful people in fantasy novels are.

You sit there and type away, and it never occurs to you that any of the characters in your book could look like you.

You're fat. You have been for as long as you can remember, and for as long as you can remember, you've been the fattest kid in school. Part of you is still in first grade, being weighed with the rest of your class for a science experiment, and you remember seeing that your number is higher than anyone else's—and not by just a little.

So, yes, you've always been fatter than everyone else in school. You know what it is to be hated for nothing more than the crime of taking up space. There were girls you'd hardly interacted with but who were cruel to you anyway. Another fat girl—smaller than you but still fat—confides in you that those girls just hate fat people. They're mean to her, too. They're not nice to anyone who isn't skinny.

You and those girls are eleven years old.

(It's too young for any of you to conceive of the idea that a body is worthy of hate just for existing.)

It's a miracle that you made it to eleven before you learned your body was a good enough reason for some to hate you.

Luckily, you have a way out. For precious minutes and stolen hours, you can escape in books. You're a reader from a family of readers. You're poor, so you can't buy that many books, but you live close enough to the library to walk there. You take a backpack and you fill it, and next week you come back to return those books and fill it again. You read and read and read.

You love science fiction and fantasy and horror. You love *Harry Potter* and *The Thief of Always* and *Dealing with Dragons*. You also love romance and drama. You've read every V. C. Andrews book your library has to offer, and you bashfully hide paperback romances among Nancy Drew and Sweet Valley High novels as if the librarian won't be scanning them individually anyway.

You read and read and read, and it will be a long time before you understand why there's a pit in your stomach every time a fat character is introduced and, inevitably, mocked. The fat characters you know are Dudley Dursley with his greedy sausage fingers, and "pleasantly plump" Bess Marvin, who never has a scene where she isn't eating. Fat characters have angry red pig faces, clumsy hands, bad memories, and food stains on their clothes. They're mean relatives who are jealous of the heroine's good looks. They mess up the hero's plans with incompetence. They're the villain the hero is fighting.

You read and read and read, and it will be a long time before you understand why there's a pit in your stomach when every heroine and leading lady is tenderly described as *slender*, as *slim*, as having a waist the hero could encircle with his hands, as delicate with long fingers. Sometimes the books will try to make it awkward, describing them as gangly and skinny, but there's always someone waiting to make them see how beautiful they are.

The Dudleys and Besses don't get that.

You don't get that.

You worry that you never will.

I know this isn't something you're thinking of when you write, but it's in us, spreading like poison. The books we read taught us by example that if a girl is going to master her magic powers, have a love triangle with a nice boy and a brooding boy (never mind you'd rather there be another girl in the mix, too), and save the world, she's going to have to be skinny.

So when you write that first novel, your heroine is skinny. She's skinny when she runs away from her oppressive home, skinny when she convinces a pirate captain to help her find her brother, skinny when you write her clumsy romantic subplot because you like reading romance more than you like writing it, skinny when she's kidnapped, skinny when she uses her wits to escape, skinny when she finds her brother and gets a happily ever after.

Months after writing that first novel, the 2007 *Hairspray* movie came out, and you'll spend years clinging to Tracy Turnblad like a lifeline. You don't know why, but I do. You haven't learned about fat oppression or fat activism. You don't even know about body positivity yet. You just know that Tracy is fat and beautiful and the hero of her story. You know that Zac Efron's Link looks at her like she's a miracle. She sings and dances not like no one is watching but like everyone *is* watching and they're lucky to be seeing her. She chases her dreams without stopping to think, "I can't do this until I've lost *x* amount of weight."

Books will take a lot longer to give you someone like Tracy. This will suck to hear, but you won't really see a fat character who makes you cry with relief until you're in college and Julie Murphy brings *Dumplin'* and Willowdean Dickson into the world. It's not fair that you have to wait that long. I wish I could give her to you now. I thought of you the whole time I was reading it and wondered what it would have been like if you'd gotten books like *Dumplin'* just a little sooner.

But right now, you're sixteen, you don't know Tracy or Willowdean, you're writing your first novel, and you don't know that a heroine can be fat.

If I could tell you anything from over a decade in the future, it would be this:

You can write the representation you're craving.

The heroine of that first novel can charm a pirate captain while she's fat. She can fatly learn about her magic, fatly sail the seas, fatly rescue her brother.

Your next NaNoWriMo novel, the one you don't finish, with the girl obsessed with flowers and their magic? She can be fat, too.

The overpowered psychic girl in novel number three? Make her fat!

Make their friends fat, too. Throw in some fat love interests.

Your fat heroine can save the world from anything—a *Reign of Fire*-style dragon apocalypse or alien invasion. She can kick ass in a red dress as well as *Resident Evil*'s Alice. She can be part of a team on a mission of questionable scientific accuracy tunneling to the center of the Earth to restart the core. All your favorite stories could have a fat girl in them.

Also, like, not to bum you out, but where I'm at, the world of science fiction and fantasy still needs a boost in fat representation. Contemporary young adult is seeing a boost—not enough of one, never enough—but the SFF side is still severely lacking.

We need you. We need *us*.

There still seems to be an idea that fat people can't lead fantasy armies or explore distant planets. Science fiction can be especially egregious about this because—as I'm sure you've noticed—when people imagine a better future, it's a future without us. It's a future where fatness is shaved away with a pill, a code, a twist to the DNA.

I know what you're feeling when you read those stories. You're wishing it could be you losing weight so easily, but at the same time, you're hurting, wondering why that would *have* to be you.

You're wondering why the you that you are couldn't stay as you are. It hurts to know that writers imagining wild, unforeseen futures can only imagine your body as something that needs fixing.

And that's *why* we need you.

You live in that body every day. We've been living in this fat body since we were small, and barring some terrible wasting disease, we're not gonna stop having this body.

OK. I know what you're thinking. (I'm you. Of course I know what you're thinking.)

You're thinking that this fatness is temporary. You just *know* that one day you're going to be skinny and beautiful and you're going to achieve your dreams.

What you don't know is that a decade from now, you're beautiful and achieving your dreams and you are fatter than you've ever been. We went to Japan and Ireland, and we did it while fat. We have the kind of friendships you can't even conceive of right now. We're in love with someone who loves us. We have our own apartment and two adorable cats. We're getting paid to write. We have agents and editors reading our essays and short stories about fat characters and asking, "Do you have more?"

We're doing all of it *while fat*.

Eventually, you're going to start writing fat characters. You're going to write short stories and novels where fat girls do amazing things.

I want you to know that while I had to wait until I was twenty-four to realize I could do that, you, Sarah? You, anyone reading this? You, at fifteen? At sixteen or seventeen or eighteen?

You can do it right now.

A year before you embarked on writing that first novel, you made a new friend. She'll be your first kiss, and she'll be the first person to tell you you're beautiful. You'll be sharing a computer during a free period, and out of the blue, she'll say your body is like a goddess's—like the Venus of Willendorf.

I know you remember that, because even though you're still struggling to believe that your body is anything other than shameful, you cling to that moment. You're in complete awe of those words and you keep them close.

I want you to take those words—that feeling—and apply it all to your characters.

Why does your heroine have to be slender? Why couldn't her silhouette be more like the Venus of Willendorf, like yours? Her stomach can roll over her thighs. Her back can be like the hilly southern Indiana landscape. Her waist doesn't need to be encompassed in two hands. She's too vast and infinite for that.

We're more infinite than that.

You're so powerful, and you don't even know it. Some of the greatest minds in writing can't imagine a future where people haven't gleefully eradicated fatness. They can't conceptualize a person being fat and making first alien contact, being fat and exploring a mystical forest, being fat and expertly wielding a sword, but *you can*.

You can write fat characters, and they don't have to be Dudley Dursley or Bess Marvin. It feels like there's a script of what characters are and you have to follow it, but I want you to rip it up. You're going off book, and you're going to create something new.

It's not always going to be easy, but it's going to free us. In all the moments when you're wondering if anyone would want to read a book where the fat girl saves the day, where she gets to be a person instead of a prop, when you're wondering if this isn't all just some kind of wish fulfillment? I want you to know that I believe in you, and I need you to write that book.

So, what are you waiting for?

Get writing.

Love,
Sarah

SARAH HOLLOWELL

is a fat Hoosier writer working to up the magic quotient of Indiana. Her work has been published on Huffington Post, *Fireside Fiction*, and *Apex*, among others. She spends an awful lot of her non-writing time listening to podcasts, playing *Breath of the Wild*, and needle felting cryptids. She can be found at sarahhollowell.com or on Twitter as @sarahhollowell.

Seven Things I Would Tell Eleven-year-old Me

by
DAVID BOWLES

ONE

You're fat.
Eres gordo.
Not "llenito" or "big-boned."
Fat.

Y no *estás* gordo,
eres gordo.
Note the verb: "eres,"
not "estás."
This fatness is not
temporary, Güero.

It's part of who you are:
a short, fat, half-Chicano,
half-white kid
with a button nose and
red hair that's already going brown.

TWO

But, man,
here's the thing—
that's totally cool.
(Wait, this is the '80s . . .
how did we say it?)
Rad. Tubular. Something.

Verás, Güerito—
you're also brilliant
and kind and cute.

Sure, I'm you and all,
hardly objective,
but others will tell you, too.
Yes, even girls.

Wait till you see your IQ,
Wait till you have learned
Your seventh language,
Wait till you get that doctorate!

The nerdiness you're starting to hate
that you want to shrug off
like a serpent's skin
along with all that fat?
Oh, dear boy,
it makes you wonderful.

Come. Come on, carajo.
Look in that mirror.
How can you call this ugly?
Your brown-orange eyes
Those dimples
That wavy hair.

You are beautiful.

THREE

Stop hating on Mexican culture.
There's nothing wrong
with your ancestors' food.

You're a mestizo kid
with genes from Europe

and Mesoamerica.
So's our family cuisine.

And it's delicious.
Steamy and rich with love . . .
your abuela's wrinkled hands
kneading the masa,
your father rolling out
his crooked tortillas.

Sure, your tíos call you gordo
(well, one ironic tía calls you flaco)
but look past the surface meaning,
see their intentions.

You are their favorite,
their gentle bookworm,
the first one to see college
as his destiny.

FOUR

I know what you—what *we*—
have planned.
It's bad. It's a mistake.
It's going to scar us.

Your body doesn't want to starve.
When we stop eating,
we're going to mess it up.
We're going to pay the price
of this fleeting skinniness
for a long time.

Oh, dear child,
get your fingers out of your mouth!
Stop! Stop!
If only I could stop you . . .

FIVE

Here's the secret
you haven't considered:
Skinny kids are unhappy, too.
Sometimes. Just like you.

Skinny kids can also feel out of place.
Their parents divorce.
Their dads leave.
They weep
alone
just
like
us.

Yes, I know. Society smiles on them.
No one looks at them
with those judging eyes.
But trust me,
a day will come
when skinny folks
will look with admiration
upon your fat frame . . .

Because they'll see it all at last,
everything you truly are—
mind, body, and soul.

SIX

Even if you weren't
supersmart and
cute like a Hobbit prince
and oh, so caring,
so ready to help, so eager
to take the weak in your arms
and carry them as far as you can . . .

You would still be worthy of love.

You are a human being,
unique and wonderful,
unlike anything that has existed
or ever will. Fat? Yes. In body
and in soul, brimming . . .

You overflow with stardust.

There is love in the world for you.
It surrounds you now. Don't you see it?
Intangible lines like a web
spread from the hearts of cousins
and tíos and abuelos and friends
and wrap you up so gently
that you barely feel
the warm gossamer
of their love.

SEVEN

I make you a solemn promise:
It gets easier.

You're going to force
thinness on that flesh,
but it knows what it wants
to be. You will be fat again.

Fat. And older. And wiser.
With a loving wife
and brilliant children.

They will throw
their arms around
your belly
and whisper
I love you.

You will wear your fat
with the pride it deserves
because it is a comfort,
a warm, soft cushion
of empathy
of compassion.

You will cradle the sadness
that threatens to crack
your loved ones
like it almost broke us

And you . . . we . . .

                                            I

I take that sorrow into my fat form
and make it fade.

DAVID BOWLES

is a Mexican American writer from the border, where he teaches at the University of Texas Rio Grande Valley and strives to perfect his decolonized chili recipe. His fifteen books—all centered on Mexican American identity, rooted in Mexico and pre-Colombian Mesoamerica—have won a bunch of cool awards, including the Pura Belpré Author Honor (twice!) and the Tomás Rivera Mexican American Children's Book Award. You can find him at davidbowles.us and @DavidOBowles on Twitter.

Black, Fat, Fem: The Weight of a Queen

by
JONATHAN P. HIGGINS, ED.D

weight

wāt/

noun

1. a body's relative mass or the quantity of matter contained by it, giving rise to a downward force; the heaviness of a person or thing.

This conversation that we are going to have is not an easy one. I realize that it is one that you've rarely had an opportunity to have, and I think it is time for us to sit down and talk about it.

Yes, my friend, you are, in fact, fat. I know it, you know it, and the world is going to constantly take any opportunity to remind you of it. The hardest part about coming to this realization won't be the things people say and do to you but your own acceptance of the fact that your journey will be complicated.

Why complicated?

Well, for starters, let's go beyond the horrific taunts of your classmates or the things you will hear and see on television. Unfortunately, much of the worst abuse that you will see and hear throughout your lifetime will be the things that live inside your own head.

For you, *fat* will always be a descriptor. A word that someone uses in front of your name to try to define your character and your worth. Someone you know will one day make a joke about your size, and you will recognize in that moment that the word is a descriptor for you, and that descriptor will cause you to go home and look in the mirror and question the worthiness of your existence.

There will forever be something about the word that bothers you. It will be a word that some use to denote the worth of your life experience, and because of that, you will more than likely go to no end to keep redefining yourself. Why? Because you will forever be taught to hate the word. Your body will begin to feel like the enemy, and you will begin to suppress the emotional pain that you bear because you will begin to believe that the pain associated with the word does not count.

Hopelessness will visit you regularly. Some days you will look to the sky and ask, "Why wasn't I given a faster metabolism?" as people shove unneeded weight-loss tips down your throat. Folks will call you the "funny friend," which you will learn is code for unattractive, because they see your weight as a problem. You might take on the role as the goofy sidekick because that is what society thinks about fat people.

Our size and the space we take up will forever be a comedic punch line—but this doesn't mean that you have to laugh along.

You will begin to feel pressured to be someone that you may have never wanted to be, questioning your self-worth. Throughout your life, others will try to equate your weight and your size to the value of your existence. But remember that you can in fact be smart, driven, beautiful, and confident, even in moments when you believe that you are undeserving.

pound·age
poundij/
noun

1. weight, especially when regarded as excessive.

There will be moments in your life when you will be tempted to hand over your power to others based off what they believe to be true about you. One of the ways that this will be done is by folks masking their fatphobia with what you might believe is a true concern for your wellness.

"Well, what about your health?" they will ask you time and time again. A physician you trust. Educators will do it. Friends and family will do it. There will be moments when you may want to give in to fear because at some point in your life, fear will in fact try to control you. Keep in mind that your health is between you and your physician and no one should have agency over how you maintain it.

Fight the urge to begin viewing your body as something separate from yourself. An enemy that you are always at war with.

Some days, you will hate skinny people: the way they look at you and the ways they treat you. You will watch them move through life with a joy that you might envy, only to learn that they, too, are not in control of their existences. There will be moments when said skinny individuals will give you backhanded compliments:

"Oh, you don't look that big" or "You look so thin today."

You will be made to feel as if you don't own your body and that your sole purpose in life is to somehow reclaim the body that you might have lost in wonderland.

Know that your mind and spirit are yours to own and that your body has the right to be centered in between the two.

whole

hōl/

adjective

1. all of; entire.

It is important to understand as you read this that there will be times in your life when it will feel like everything is centered on your size. How you give love; how you receive it. Some days will be easier than others, and some days you will ask yourself, "Why does the world hate me simply because I am larger than others?"

As you begin to think about the meaning of your existence, I want to remind you that being fat doesn't mean you deserve any less. Being fat does not mean you are less of anything. It means you have carried more, and there is so much more to your life.

Some days, you will feel like you don't deserve to be loved. That you are not valuable and that you are not entitled to fulfilling moments of life, love, and friendships.

Never let the weight you carry make you feel as if you are not whole.

You don't need to wait to be skinny to live your life to the fullest. Your weight doesn't and will never hold you back. Continue to walk and speak in full totality. You are not your size.

Please don't allow someone to make you feel like there isn't any value to your voice because of how much space you take up. You deserve everything, if not more, for who you are and what you have been through.

Your existence is not a reflection of your weight.

Your worth is not determined by your poundage.

You have been and will always be whole.

JONATHAN P. HIGGINS, ED.D

is a Black, fat, femme freelance journalist, speaker, and thought leader who examines the intersections of gender, race, and media. Their work has been featured on sites including Think Progress, *Essence*, *Out* magazine, them, Into, and more. They hold a doctorate in educational justice and write regularly about Black LGBTQ+ liberation and what it means to not just survive, but thrive. You can follow them on all social media outlets by using the handle @DoctorJonPaul.

The 5 Things You Need to Start Your Very Own Rad Fat Babe Revolution

(from Someone Who Knows)

by
VIRGIE TOVAR

Have you ever seen a fat person wearing a tiny bathing suit and swimming in the ocean? I have! Have you ever seen a fat person walking down a runway in lingerie? I have! Have you ever watched a band of fat people singing songs about quesadillas? I have!

I didn't know that fat people could live rad, joyful, stylish, amazing, revolutionary, inspiring lives until I started hanging out with fat people who were living rad, joyful, stylish, amazing, revolutionary, inspiring lives.

I remember the exact moment that changed my life forever: I was at a conference for fat people in Oakland, California. Imagine me: At the time I was kind of frumpy, my glasses were not exactly the right size, and I wore far too many dark blue clothes. I walked into the conference hotel and saw a group of fat people hanging out at the pool. They were laughing, napping, chatting, applying sunscreen, eating snacks, floating on inner tubes, making out, wearing supercute bathing suits and generally having a damn good time. I had never seen anything like this! It was my dream come true—except I'd been taught by our fatphobic culture and mass media that those kinds of dreams only came true if you were thin. And then something even more miraculous happened! I saw this glamorous woman with a big belly and big thighs saunter into the pool area. She was wearing cat-eye sunglasses and a vintage red-and-white polka-dot bikini. She looked like a 1950s celebrity except fat. And trailing behind her was a boy who was carrying a parasol over her head, so she wouldn't get a sunburn.

I was taught by society that only thin people have amazing lives. Maybe you've been taught this, too. Our culture tries hard to make you think this is true. And so I spent most of my life hating my body, wishing I looked different, eating too little food, doing a whole lot of unnecessarily painful exercise routines rather than seeking out activities I truly enjoyed, and waiting for my life to start. Well, I'm going to tell you a secret: You have the right to an amazing life on your terms at any size. You don't have to wait to be smaller. *Start now at whatever size you are.* And I'm here to share five of my favorite tips for starting your very own rad fat babe revolution.

Ready?

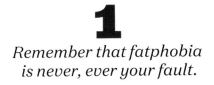

Remember that fatphobia is never, ever your fault.

Fatphobia is a form of bigotry or discrimination, like homophobia, sexism, or racism. Many people instantly know that homophobia, sexism, and racism are problems. However, it can be harder for people to understand that the way we treat fat people is a problem—even though it really, really is! Here's the thing: When people treat you poorly based on what you look like or what you weigh, that's a form of abuse. Abuse is never the fault of the victim and is always the fault of the abuser. It's easy for us to accept blame for our abuse, because we're taught that we can make the abuse stop if we just—*poof!*—lose weight. This is called *victim blaming*. The truth is that it's much, much easier for a jerk to stop being a jerk than for a fat person to become a thin person. Someone can choose to stop being a bigot—instant results guaranteed. The same isn't true for a person's weight.

Find and create amazing fat representation.

I have a double chin (DC for short) and chubby cheeks, and it's important for me to defy the chins-phobia I see all around me. I don't like taking pictures of myself from above. I take pictures of myself from below to show off my bangin' DC. One thing that affects the way you feel about yourself is what you're seeing. I highly recommend being very intentional about what you're reading and what you're seeing. Check in with your body and gauge how you're reacting to what you're seeing. If something—like a magazine, TV show, or a social media account—makes you feel icky about yourself, stop engaging with it immediately. I mean it! Fill your feed with images and ideas that lift you up, not tear you down. That aforementioned thing called *social media*—I'm sure you've heard of it—is essentially a free publishing tool. A couple years ago I directed this short film called *Machete Babes*. It was a feminist horror movie about fat babes getting revenge against killer vegetables. We made it on our phones, edited it on iMovie, and put it up on YouTube. A long time ago, only a few people had access to media publishing. It was expensive, and people worked really hard to get enough fame or money to be able to publish their ideas. Now you can write, direct, or post an image from pretty much anywhere in the world at no cost. Use the ability to share the things that inspire you to create the kind of representation you want to see.

3

Wear what you want.

Fat people face unique challenges around fashion because we're taught that the only thing we should do with clothes is use them to cover up our bodies. Thin people are likelier to be encouraged to use fashion for self-expression, while fat people are taught that self-expression is off-limits. Total lie! Each and every human has a unique perspective, style, and gender presentation. Fat people can use fashion differently than thin people because we have a bigger "canvas" to play with. For example, I love wearing huge earrings and very large prints. I feel that my bigger body lends itself perfectly to these larger pieces. We've been taught to see straight lines and angularity as normal, but my body brings something different to the table—roundness and soft lines. For a really long time I felt pressure to wear big and bulky sweaters, dark colors, and oversize pants to cover my shape. This look works for some people, but it didn't work for me. I wanted to wear neon, floral prints, pink lipstick, pencil skirts, crop tops, bodycon dresses, bikinis, and big jewelry. That's *my* style. That's what makes me feel the most like myself. I encourage you to figure out what makes you feel most like yourself and wear it proudly—not for anyone else but for YOU.

4
Have high standards for who gets to be in your life.

I remember growing up and being close friends with people who never stood up for me and who sometimes even criticized me and talked negatively about my body. We all deserve better than that. You have the right to have friends who really *see* you and help you feel safe, not people who are going to regulate you or refuse to show up for you. Sometimes we have to teach our friends—or even our family members—to be the people we need them to be. I recommend taking a few days to figure out what you want from the people who are closest to you (e.g., "I want the people closest to me to encourage me to love myself" or "I want the people closest to me not to encourage me to go on a diet"). Practice what you might say in these conversations so you're more confident about what you are asking of your friends and family. Tell them about these expectations, give them some time (maybe one or two months) to adjust, and then start creating some emotional distance from those who aren't ready to show up for you.

5

Don't ever date someone who thinks you need to lose weight.

I used to believe that I had to lose weight if I wanted someone to love me or date me. I thought that I was ruining my love life because I failed at losing weight. The problem with that logic is (1) Fat people have relationships and fall in love and get married and get into polyamorous relationships all the time; (2) Anyone who dates someone based on their body size is not worth dating. You're not missing ANYTHING by being your current body size. People who need their partner to look a certain way are insecure and afraid. They're not interested in getting close to someone and truly loving someone. They're interested in controlling their partners and using their romantic partners to level up and get recognition from their friends and others who subscribe to our fatphobic culture. You're worth more than that. When you really expect and demand respect—especially if you're a woman or feminine person—you are totally going to come up against resistance. We're socialized to date whoever will date us and stay with them no matter how crappy it is. That's not very fun, in my experience. It will take longer to find a partner; but trust me, it's really worth the wait.

Now you've got a starter kit to brew your very own little revolution at home. Congratulations, friend! I want to end by reminding you how powerful you are. This culture—and the boring jerks who are here to uphold it—try to make us feel powerless and voiceless every single day. That's a bummer, but you have many tools and plenty of magic. Keep proclaiming that magic in the face of naysayers. Go boldly forward in the pursuit of your big, fat dreams.

ANDRIA LO

VIRGIE TOVAR

was named one of the fifty most influential feminists by *Bitch* magazine in 2018. She is the author of *You Have the Right to Remain Fat* and is an activist and one of the nation's leading experts and lecturers on fat discrimination and body image. She started the hashtag campaign #LoseHateNotWeight. Find her on Instagram and Twitter @virgietovar.

I Wear What I Want 'Cause I Want To

by
P. S. KAGUYA

When I was younger all I could think was, When can I be pretty so I can be accepted? Back then *pretty* meant being skinny. I'd think, Will I ever be a size zero? It seemed like all the girls who wore Abercrombie & Fitch or Hollister all looked the same and smelled the same and were able to get all the hot guys. I thought they had everything. But I also had to wonder: Were these girls really happy, or were they just acting like it?

If only I'd known how beautiful I was when I was younger. It's true that having supportive parental figures is helpful in building your self-esteem. But parents are not always perfect, and they also have their own insecurities. This is not me saying, "Parents are the worst." This is just a reminder not to let even an adult judge you for how you look. Most folks project negativity toward someone because they have their own insecurities. Don't let those impact you.

One thing I wish I could tell myself as a teenager: Things do get better. None of the people who bullied you will matter in ten years. They will never be like you or have the experiences and the joy of being unapologetically you.

As a teenager, I listened to the ghost whispers of me not being good enough. They said, *You are NOT SKINNY* a.k.a. NOT PRETTY enough to get anything you want. *You are FAT. You are NOT HEALTHY.* But ultimately it wasn't my appearance that people fell in love with. In adulthood, I've found that it is mainly my energy. My confidence.

Confidence? What does that even mean? How can I be confident? Some people purchase their confidence via material goods like clothes, electronics, jewelry, or makeup. Some perform extremely well academically, and others perform in front of crowds by acting, singing, and playing music. Still others do sports or hang with their friends. But not everyone has to *do* a particular thing in order to feel confident.

What are some ways I work on my own confidence? I remember looking at my mirror and wondering why I was never good enough. But a new habit I've developed over the years is, when looking in the mirror, acknowledging that it's just another day to conquer! Repeating mantras to yourself is a good practice and one of the first steps you can take toward SELF-LOVE. Try writing in a notebook or diary just to talk about your day—you are expressing yourself, which is awesome! This can be an outlet of some sort and can reduce any inner negativity.

Once in high school, I wore a short denim skort, thinking it would be cute; but then the whole day I felt like everyone was staring at my fat legs. I was hyperaware of my stomach bulging when I sat down. In hindsight I realize no one was looking—no one at all. It was all in my head!

With occasional exceptions like the above, I typically wore baggy pants and T-shirts during my youth. I grew up in a conservative family household and was constantly told to cover up. I didn't have access to clothing that was cute or fit right. I heard so many negative comments as a teenager, both from family and kids in school: "You shouldn't wear white, because it makes you look bigger." Or, "You need to wear longer sleeves to cover up your fat arms." Or, "Look at those thunder thighs and that full-moon ass." I absorbed these taunts like a sponge. I digested them until I felt I wasn't good enough for anyone.

I allowed myself to become mired in insecurity because I was trying *so hard* to fit in, when what I should have been doing was telling myself how beautiful I was and how much I loved who I'd become. I didn't need to be like everyone else in order to love myself. Ultimately *you* hold the only opinion that matters! Don't try to change yourself in order to be accepted. And if you ever do want change, then you know that change is for you, not anyone else.

I never saw myself as anyone important—that's not what it was about. Importance and clout are so obsolete. Being genuine and understanding are the most important traits in the journey of self-love. As I reach the end of my twenties, I am the biggest I've ever been and by far the happiest I've been. Happiness is worth striving for, but it is *not* directly correlated to size.

I hope my story can help you! Your perceptions won't change in a blink of an eye, but to change anything, you must first acknowledge and reflect. Take time to be alone, and take moments to admire yourself. You are beautiful the way you are.

Love,

P. S. Kaguya

P. S. Loving myself has been the best thing that has ever happened to me. <3

P. S. KAGUYA

is a plus-size curve model and sex-positive influencer and ambassador based in New York City. She has two guinea pigs, loves cute things, and watches cartoons and anime. She also has a background in photography, music, and cosmetology and found her voice by starting a WordPress site, which then progressed into using Instagram. Her self-love journey inspired her and her audience to the point that she pursued modeling full-time, and she is forever fighting and aiming for inclusiveness in the modeling world, NOT ONLY as a model but as a first-generation Korean American.

Fatness & Horror: The Match Made in Not Heaven

by
HILLARY MONAHAN

"And why am I alive when everyone around me has turned to meat? It's because of my list of rules. Rule number one for surviving Zombieland: cardio. When the virus struck, for obvious reasons, the first ones to go were the fatties."
[Insert the screaming of a fat man as a zombie overcomes him and devours him on a football field with the voiceover of, "Poor fat bastard."]

—Zombieland, 2009

Zombieland is a movie I enjoyed tremendously . . . after I got past the opening gut punch, when the dude who'd one day play Lex Luthor (poorly) suggested in his inaugural guffaw that fats like me die first because, essentially, we deserve it. We don't do cardio, after all—as though all thin people do and thus are better equipped to survive. It's a careless statement, and insensitive, and patently false; but the low-hanging fruit was there, and screenwriters Rhett Reese and Paul Wernick decided it'd be OK to take the shot because it'd only impact *some* of the people in the audience who shelled out money to see the film, not all.

People have been conditioned to laugh at fat bodies—to see them as jokes worthy of ridicule—for a long time. And, as comedy and horror have been intertwined for longer than many of us have been alive (*Abbott and Costello Meet Frankenstein* came out in 1948, for example), you're going to see an overlap. Comedy is, after all, a perfect way to deescalate a tense, horrific situation. But horror is intrinsically violent, so when you have the baseline premise that fat bodies are jokes *and* a trusty wood chipper nearby, what better way to rack up your body count than to shove the fatty in headfirst and to see what happens? No one *really* cares, right? It's just another dead fat person, and they court death on their own with every bite of food they take.

Don't believe that this is a thing? Watch the most egregious example of this in yet another favorite film of mine, *Trick 'r Treat* (2007). You'll meet Charlie, the lone fat character in the whole movie with a name. When he reads a sign left on his principal's porch instructing guests to take only one piece of candy from the offerings, of course he takes a handful (because fat people can't resist food), and the principal emerges from the house just in time for a casual mention of diabetes.

Before quite literally poisoning him to death and decapitating him.

If that doesn't convince you, rewind to the completely terrifying movie *Se7en* (1995), where the gluttony murder is a fat man tied to a chair who is forced to eat until his stomach explodes. His fatness is on gruesome display, along with the mountains of food before him. It's supposed to shock and disgust you. It accomplishes both; but for fat people, the disgust is often far more complicated because we know on some level that the horror for the thin people in the audience is the fatness itself, not what's being done to the fat victim on the screen.

We, the fats, are the monster.

At least with *Se7en* it's only a suggestion. The year 2006 saw the early James Gunn release *Slither*, which—with Nathan Fillion and Elizabeth Banks in its cast—should have been a winner for me. I enjoy both actors. The fact that it was billed as a horror comedy also worked in its favor—my favorite movie is *Young Frankenstein*, after all. Ultimately it failed on two fronts: the sex assault (a character is victimized by the alien-man played by Michael Rooker against a funny, feel-good, hoedown background) *and* its eventual, disastrous portrayal of fatness. Post assault, the character of Brenda transforms from a thin woman into a massive, rotund breeder, her swollen body on garish display. It's exploitive, it's awful, and when she explodes in a sea of fat and gook and monster babies, I flinched—because once again, a round person was portrayed as the horrific thing.

It's glaringly obvious that horror has made fatness into a morality tale. Being fat is the thing you do or choose that justifies punishment. Just like Little Red Riding Hood shouldn't have talked to strangers, the fat person shouldn't be so blatantly fat. They're essentially asking for it. This is a trope itself, much like the girl who goes all the way being murder fodder or, until recently and with the rise of great filmmakers like Jordan Peele, the person of color dying first.

What's interesting here is that the exploitation of fat bodies in horror is a relatively new phenomenon (starting in the 1990s onward) that actually makes a lot of sense. When I was poking around for academic papers about fat characters on TV and film, I found one called "All the News that's Fat to Print: The American 'Obesity Epidemic' and the Media" by sociologist Natalie Boero. Boero traces the rise of anti-fat sentiment starting in 1990 all the way through 2001. She read more than 750 articles showing how we went from casual condemnation of fatness to focusing on it as a health crisis. Boero found it only took ten years to take fatness from a lesser talking point to a major one. What does that tell us? It means horror wasn't always like this, because society wasn't always like this.

Bigger translation? Before the nineties, fats faced a totally different problem than the convenient-victim one. We simply didn't exist in any serious guise. Not on mainstream TV, not in film or fiction—and that includes horror.

Maybe you remember I mentioned Lou Costello. He was fat, right? But Costello is the exception, not the rule, and he benefits from being a comedian. Funny fat people have al-

We need more fat creators to tell their own stories.

ways been an acceptable norm, particularly if they're willing to make fat jokes. The comedy/horror overlap is a niche one, though, so if you look at horror films predating the nineties, and separate out the comedies, you're going to see almost nonexistent representation. Outside of Kathy Bates in 1990's *Misery* (and she's the antagonist), we don't exist. Or, if we do, we're background noise. With the exception of Vance Norris from 1982's *The Thing*, the horror we know as classics excludes us. Don't believe it? Let's take a look at some of the best-known horror films:

The Exorcist
Nosferatu
The Shining
A Nightmare on Elm Street
Friday the 13th
Rosemary's Baby
Night of the Living Dead
Any of the universal horror greats.

No fat people to be seen. But as we know, fat people have always been around. I guess the question is: Is it better for the world to pretend you don't exist, or is it better to be zombie snacks?

Suffice to say, it's not easy to be a horror fan and a fat person. But I have hope. While some media still rely on the tired "fats as monster fodder" thing, we also are starting to see ourselves represented not just as trusty sidekicks, but as central protagonists. The first example that comes to mind is Nick Frost from Edgar Wright's *Shaun of the Dead* (2004). In Frost's character, Ed, we have the (admittedly problematic) trope of the slovenly fat guy, an unemployed layabout who only plays video games, mooches off his friends, and eats crap food. Sure, we've seen that before. But then the world ends, zombies rise and start attacking, and Ed . . . Ed reveals himself to be the most noble, heroic protagonist I've seen in a horror film in a long time. Ed kicks zombie ass and his body doesn't have to change at all. He is a loyal, funny, and brave fat character who is more than zombie bait.

Another example of the fat guy winning is found in 2010's *Tucker & Dale vs. Evil*, starring Alan Tudyk and Tyler Labine. Labine plays the warm, simplehearted Dale, a fat guy in a trucker hat who just wants to have a great vacation in the woods with his best friend. This film is one of my favorites because it actively subverts a lot of problematic horror tropes, playing with our (often classist) notions of southern rural life and flipping off The Man by shining light on the rarely celebrated heroic fat guy. Yes, Labine is funny, and yes, he's also portrayed as a bit of a slob, but ultimately, he's the winner. He beats the bad guys. And even better? He scores the girl.

A fat character getting a love interest and romantic arc shouldn't be so revolutionary in this day and age, and yet, here we are.

The glaringly obvious *thing* with these two examples is that they are both allocishet white men (white men who are not queer), but it had to start somewhere, and I feel like they paved the way for the horror media that has come since. I've been discussing film to this point, but I'd be remiss not to mention the rise of *American Horror Story*, in particular *Coven* and its inclusion of fat women. In *American Horror Story: Coven,* set in New Orleans and following a coven of witches throughout the years, Kathy Bates is back in all her scene-eating glory as the hideous Delphine LaLaurie. But the far more impressive presence, to me, was Gabourey Sidibe blessing our lives with her portrayal of Queenie, the living voodoo doll. Gabourey is fat, she's beautiful, she's Black, and she stole the show. What's noteworthy here is that this isn't a comedy, so the fat character wasn't reduced to slapstick or visual laughs. While there are facets of the representation that I didn't care for (in particular, there's a scene showing Queenie as so romantically desperate, she tries to seduce a minotaur), there are other aspects, including how severely badass she is, that resonated beautifully.

Horror comedy once again delivered on its fat rep in 2016, this time with Melissa Mc-Carthy in *Ghostbusters: Answer the Call.* The next year, we saw Lil Rel Howery playing the hilarious and heroic Rod in *Get Out,* which was a brilliant, sobering film; but Rod's comedic timing and presence gave us the breath of fresh air we needed to recover from Peele's onslaught of scares.

In 2017 Octavia Spencer played Zelda in *The Shape of Water,* which, while categorized as a drama, is still a reimagining of *The Creature from the Black Lagoon* so I'm stealing it for the horror category. Octavia is another beautiful fat Black woman whose presence in a horror film is revolutionary compared to the body of work that came before. Were there issues with the character and the film itself? Yes, and it's worth discussing the issues with the ableist and racist elements of the story, but casting Spencer at all was a victory in some ways, albeit a victory with asterisks. I hope we can and will do better by all fat people, but particularly by fat people of color.

This is not a comprehensive list of representation by any stretch of the imagination, but it is a pie slice of examples to give you an idea of the scope of our struggles as fat people in this genre, how far we have come over the years, and how far we still have to go. While I can honestly say I think we will see more fat characters given roles that explore actual fat existence thanks to fat activism (including but not limited to being gainfully employed! In relationships! As parents!

As athletes! As not slobs!), horror has its work cut out for it to climb out of its hole. Realistically, until horror creators can accept that fat reality *isn't* in itself horrific—until it's just a state of being for many people, just like having blue or brown eyes—it'll fail fat people.

Does this mean creators should just not include fat people in horror? Erasure is never an answer for any marginalized group in mainstream media, fats included, and horror included. As a fat horror writer, I believe the key to effective fat representation, even in violent or horrific situations, is an egalitarian hand. Make victims out of your fat folks *just like you would everyone else.* Not because of their fatness. Not for a laugh so the audience can snicker at the fat guy who can't outrun the murderer because a writer makes a false equivalency between thinness and health. Let's try some revolutionary thinking here: How about some acknowledgment that fat people are often super strong in no small part because of the weight they carry? That seems like a good quality to have in times of danger, doesn't it?

We need more fat creators to tell their own stories. That's part of what I'm doing: putting fat characters into the horror I create. We need more fat teenagers being fantastic and brave. Show us intersectional fat folks—like queer fats and fats of color, or both! Create some superamazing fat villains without making them slobs, as is the genre tendency. Have some fat love interests so the stakes of danger for your main characters are higher!

There are so many ways to include fat people in horror arcs and stories that won't diminish us, attack our dignity, or feed the ugly stereotypes that reduce us to jokes or meat fodder, and none of those ways gut the actual horror element from our films and media. We're not there yet, but I have hope, particularly with the rise of fat artists in my own circles in young adult literature. Are you a fat teen who is a huge horror fan? You can put yourself into the story. Make the movie where you slay vampires, or write the book where you survive the haunted house. If you're a fat teen and you love horror, know that you can be part of the fat revolution. See yourself as the hero, the survivor, or even the monster, just the size you are.

As the fat discourse improves—as we see more representation—fat people, too, can enjoy our time in the pile of bloody bodies. This may not seem like a great goal to some, but for us horror fans, the idea of being with our peers—and *rotting* with our peers, for no other reason than being in the wrong place at the wrong time—is fantastic.

HILLARY MONAHAN

is the *New York Times* bestselling author of the YA horror novel *MARY: The Summoning* and, under the pen name Eva Darrows, the critically acclaimed *The Awesome* and *Dead Little Mean Girl*. A multigenre author, Hillary writes everything from horror and comedy to science fiction and fantasy and romance for young adult and adult audiences alike.

A Poem That's About Nature and Fatness

by
MIGUEL M. MORALES

No one shames a pond for being too wide.

"All you do is sit around all day reflecting.

You need to move around. Get your water flowing.

Be more active like your cousin, the river, it runs *every day*."

No one tells a field of wildflowers it should wear black

because it's slimming or that it should stay away from bright

colors or that those petal patterns it displays make it look fat.

"Oh, what a shame because you have such a pretty face."

No one tries to belittle a tree for having a thick trunk.

They don't snatch fruit from its broad branches saying,

"You've had enough already" or "I'm just trying to help."

It's a fucking tree. It has willpower and the rings to prove it.

Our fatness is natural, yet it's often judged, not unlike clouds.

When dark, low, and tempestuous, people shake their heads.

When light, bright, and fluffy, people smile at it, amused.

Whether it blankets the sky or is nowhere to be found,

Our fatness is as natural as

a cloud,

a pond,

a field,

of wild

flowers

and, yes,

even a tree.

MIGUEL M. MORALES

grew up working as a migrant/seasonal farmworker. He now works in a library, filling his day with students and words but mostly clearing paper jams. Miguel's fat writings appear in *Hibernation and other Poems by Bear Bards, Imaniman: Poets Writing in the Anzalduan Borderlands, From Macho to Mariposa: New Gay Latino Fiction*, and in Brian Kornell's limited essay series Fat and Queer, *Queen Mob's Teahouse.* You can find Miguel as @TrustMiguel on Facebook, Twitter, and Instagram.

For the Love of Ursula's Revenge Body

by
JULIE MURPHY

The first movie I have a very clear memory of seeing in theaters was Disney's *The Little Mermaid*. It was love at first sight. Not just with *The Little Mermaid*, but with the experience of seeing a movie in a dark room full of strangers, the smell of butter and sweet soda syrup in the air. I lived in Connecticut at the time and had just turned four years old. I remember walking outside and finding that the sun had set during our time in the theater. To my four-year-old self, the whole experience felt magical but in a definitively grown-up kind of way.

I wish I could tell you that I fell in love with Ursula (not just the experience of moviegoing) at first sight and that even as a child, she worked her magic on me. I wish I could say she immediately taught me—a chubby Irish girl sitting in a dark movie theater—that my body could be great and powerful and beautiful, if only I could see all that in myself.

As we walked to our car that night after the movie, I yanked on my mother's arm and begged her to take me back inside so I could experience the whole thing again. Whether it was *The Little Mermaid* or the moviegoing experience itself, I'm really not sure, but one thing was for certain: I wanted to be a princess just like Ariel. I wanted two sea creature best friends, a fork in my hair, a suave prince—the whole thing. The best part was, I was too young and naïve to know that most people would call a fat girl foolish for even thinking she could dream of those things.

Now I'm an adult who—thanks to my lovely nieces—has been subjected to watching *Frozen* and *Moana* enough times that they've been drilled into my head permanently. This has allowed me to appreciate the patience exhibited by every adult in my life when *The Little Mermaid* was released on VHS. (For the record, *Frozen* and *Moana* are iconic.) When I was a kid, the VHS release of your favorite movie was an event, especially if it was a Disney movie and came in one of those puffy cases that almost felt like you were holding a storybook. (If you're too young for this, do a quick Internet search and walk down the memory lane that is my childhood.) It wasn't long before I had *The Little Mermaid* committed to memory.

It took me a few years before I was jaded enough to look a little more closely at the fat characters of my childhood. To me, Ursula had always just been the scary evil sea witch who happened to be fat, and nothing about that felt significant.

First, a little on me and my fat-girl history: I've always been fat. The childhood obesity epidemic that the news always talked about with accompanying images of headless, anonymous fat kids? That was me they were referring to. In fact, I'll never forget hearing that phrase for the first time—"childhood obesity epidemic." It was from a school nurse who was giving a presentation to my class. I immediately felt her zeroing in on me, like I was the villain. I was patient zero, and the disease they couldn't contain was my fatness. Around the time I became aware of my fatness, so did my classmates. Suddenly the first insult slung at me during playground spats wasn't about my family or falling asleep in class. It was about my body. I wasn't just stupid. I was fat and stupid. Or fat and lazy. Fat and gross. Fat and smelly.

It took a few more years of harsh fat-girl realities before I could fully appreciate Ursula. Over time, as my body became the first weapon utilized by people looking to hurt me, Ursula became this villain who scared me in a new way. (Yes, there were other plus-size villainesses who came before Ursula [s/o to the Queen of Hearts! Off with their heads, girl.], but no one made me uncomfortable in the way Ursula did.) I wasn't scared that she would steal my voice or my charming prince. I found something new to be scared of. And this time it was the way Ursula embraced her body with her fatty back rolls and her revealing dress. That was wrong. She wasn't supposed to hold her head up high, and she definitely wasn't supposed to be delighted in her body. Right? Have you ever seen someone walking with purpose when you feel like you're fumbling, just trying to get your footing? That was how Ursula made me feel for a season of my life. Either the bitch had all the answers, or she was really good at faking it.

Of course, Ursula is fictional, so I found myself digging a little deeper into the inspiration behind Ursula so that maybe I could understand why she made me feel simultaneously intrigued and uneasy. A quick Internet search showed that the inspiration behind the sea witch with the mostest is the John Waters muse and icon, Divine. In case you don't know who Divine is, she was a drag queen from Baltimore who played Tracy Turnblad's mother in the original *Hairspray*. She was crude and gross and funny and fat and even a little bit sexy—even if you didn't want to admit it. I could write pages about power dynamics and privilege between both fat women and gay men, but for the sake of this essay, I'll just say that fat women and gay men have often found common ground and bonded over being rule breakers. Fat women don't play by society's rule that a woman's body exists solely for male gratification, and gay men subvert the gender roles that men have traditionally relied on for the purpose of keeping women and people of color out of power. Like I said, there's so much more nuance to consider, but the point is: OF COURSE URSULA WAS INSPIRED BY A DRAG QUEEN. Of course she challenged me and made me uncomfortable. That's what she was designed to do.

She was crude and gross and funny and fat and even a little bit sexy.

We never have the good fortune of seeing Ursula's backstory play out on-screen, but something about her tells you she's a woman scorned. And yet, rather than turning into the expected (a dowdy shrew), she became a ravishing fat sea witch. As someone who loves both stories and fat people, I constantly find myself homing in on how fat people are portrayed. There are a lot of fat tropes we see over and over again, and one that Ursula so artfully subverts is *the revenge body*. The revenge body trope asserts that for a fat woman to avenge herself and to prove to her bullies once and for all that they were wrong about her, she must lose weight. Only then will her vengeance be fully realized. Essentially, the fat woman must become something she is not to prove that she was worthy all along. Not Ursula though. With her tentacles, back rolls, and red lips, Ursula isn't waiting for a revenge body. She already has one. For Ursula, her fat body is her revenge body, just as it should be. What if we all stopped waiting to be someone else and instead just embraced the people we are in the bodies we have? We'd be unstoppable.

My love affair with Ursula has been a slow, needling thing in the same way my love affair with my own body has been. The more I come to accept myself, the more Ursula means to me. Ursula's is the kind of fat that's in your face and is a giant middle finger to anyone who dares cross her, which is why the year I decided to go as Ursula for Halloween—my absolute favorite holiday—will always stand out to me. It sounds silly, I know, but choosing to go as Ursula for Halloween was a big step for me. It was one of the first times I very blatantly acknowledged that *Yes, I am fat!* Ursula is so defined by her body and the shape of it that something about dressing as her for Halloween felt like a challenge to anyone who had ever accused me of being an epidemic or used the word *fat* to bully me. I've gone on a long journey to take back my body from all the people who have used it against me. There have been landmark moments along the way, such as reclaiming the word *fat,* swearing off diets in favor of intuitive eating, and learning to find joy in movement and exercise instead of pain and punishment. But that night as I danced with all my friends (some of them in drag)—my hair sprayed white and my skin slathered in purple body paint—will always be a physical manifestation of how far I've come in learning that my fat body is a very good body. I sauntered through that Halloween party with my flabby arms and double chin,

letting my body speak for itself and never once underestimating the importance of body language.

JULIE MURPHY

lives in North Texas with her husband, who loves her; her dog, who adores her; and her cats, who tolerate her. After several wonderful years in the library world, Julie now writes full time. When she's not writing or reliving her reference-desk glory days, she can be found watching made-for-TV movies, hunting for the perfect slice of cheese pizza, or planning her next great travel adventure. She is also the author of the young adult novels *Puddin'*, *Ramona Blue*, *Side Effects May Vary*, and *Dumplin'* (now a Netflix original film). *Dear Sweet Pea* is her first book for middle-grade readers.

You can visit Julie at juliemurphywrites.com.

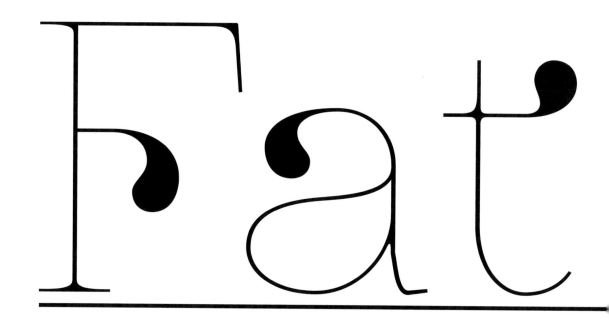

Fat

by
SHELBY BERGEN

I t's always been my goal to depict fat bodies as they are, existing and living their lives. I started drawing fat bodies because I didn't see anyone who looked like me in any of the art I enjoyed. So I started drawing myself and drawing other bodies that looked like mine. That's my favorite thing about being an artist: When I want something to exist, I can make it exist. I have the power in my own two hands to make something exist just because I want it to. You have this power, too. It felt powerful, and still does, to depict myself and people with bodies like mine in a loving and honest way. I continue to do it in the hopes that others feel empowered by my work: whether it's to wear that pretty dress, go to that cool event, or do that thing they're so scared of doing.

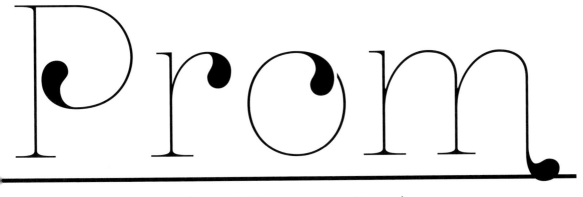

Prom

(an illustration)

I chose to create a piece about prom because prom always felt like a party I was never invited to. Being fat took all the fun out of school dances for me, because who was going to ask me to go with them? Would the dress shops my thin friends shopped at have my size, too? How do you even dance, like, in general? So I never even went to most school dances. I personally never even had a prom experience—not because I didn't go, but because the arts high school I went to had something that was vaguely shaped like prom but definitely was not prom. So all my prom references come from movies like *Footloose* and *10 Things I Hate About You*. These films depicted prom as the epitome of the high school experience, but all their prom scenes were lacking in representation, especially when it came to fat bodies. I wanted to create a piece that showed fat bodies moving and joyous and dancing and not worrying about any of the things that I worried about when it came to school dances. I wanted to draw fat teens— wanted to draw people like you—who felt like they were invited to the prom party, too.

SHELBY BERGEN

is a freelance illustrator, body positive advocate, and world champion cat petter from the frigid land of Minneapolis. She uses her work to advocate for body diversity and inclusivity in modern illustration and other commercial art. You can find her and all of her work online at shelbybergen.com, on Instagram @shelby.bergen, and on Twitter @shelbobergen.

Fat and Thriving

---

by
ISABEL QUINTERO

See, your body never stops changing. Ever.
It is a magnificent thing. In all its rolls and
all its jiggles. It is a beautiful thing. Sometimes though

    my body feels
    like a chore
    like it does not belong to me
    my limbs my panza
    just weights to keep myself tethered
    to the ground

    sometimes it's like other hands
    hold my body up
    or down
    hands that do not belong to me
    touching and molding what isn't theirs

    usurping the shape of my skin.

The first time I realized I was fat was in the fourth grade. My mom told me I looked like a pregnant woman. I went to school the next day and asked friends if I looked pregnant to them. I remember that as the moment my weight shifted in my brain into something important. I don't hold it against my mom. At least not now. Though I used to. I really did. What I've come to learn now is that parents are simply people who are trying their best, and therefore will mess up. Often. I've learned that my mom is a cis woman like me, and as such, she was teaching me how to survive as a woman when much of the value we have is put into how we look. Especially in terms of finding a mate—something that's always stressed for me. Now, my mom, like most folks who love us do, framed the push to lose weight as being healthy. It was always about health. Health, health, health. And to be honest, I believed her because she's my mom and worried about me. Remember, she was teaching me how to survive. And because of her upbringing my mother is a hell of a survivor. To her, being healthy and beautiful was part of how you survived as a cis woman.

If you've read my first book, *Gabi, a Girl in Pieces,* you may remember the section where Gabi makes a list of questions she wants to ask her mom but is too afraid to ask. Perhaps you have a list of similar questions anxious to be asked but know that's not going to happen because opening your mouth and letting them out may come with consequences or shame. Gabi's list of questions is also a list of questions that as a teen I wanted to ask my mom.

I was raised to be independent
but to need
a man. to want to have a man.
not a woman. a man.
because men are strong
they can do things we can't
because women are not enough
on their own.

my mom's friend warned that
my growing waistline
my lack of lipstick
would scare my husband into
the arms of some thin thing
who knew how to use her mouth
to say sweet things
that slipped out tinted red or pink.
I was never asked if I even liked sugar.

Before I was married, I was a teen who was lost in her own body. I remember telling my best friend in high school, "If I ever hit two hundred pounds, kill me." I'm glad she forgot because I would've been dead years ago. I think of that now and am ashamed of how much I hated that body. I would like to go back and tell teenage Isabel how amazing she was and how powerful her body could be if she simply accepted it as hers. Because despite looking in a mirror that for so long only reflected what I didn't like about my body or what others saw could be changed, I more often than not am able to see how complete I really am.

When I was asked to write something for this anthology, I was excited. But then I had a moment that many of us who are fat go through—doubt of our magnificence. It happens and it's shitty. It's painful and discouraging. It makes me question the validity of what I had to say to you, young person who is learning to love their body as a given and not on someone else's terms on what that love should look like or at what size it's OK to love that body. I talked to my friend, and poet, Allyson Jeffredo, and she said, "Write that! It's vulnerable and real. One will never feel 100 percent about their body in this world." She was right. Loving our bodies, especially our fat bodies, especially fat bodies of color, fat queer bodies of color, is never easy. I recognize that as a light-skinned Chicana I have privileges that my darker skinned hermanx are often not afforded. White people, in many of the spaces I move through (publishing, education, coffeeshops), seem to be real comfortable around me until I open my mouth. Sometimes a shift happens in the conversation when the Mexican jumps out my mouth.

A step back. A reassessment. I become a little exotic. A different kind of Mexican than the one they expected.

I was once at a hot springs (I had convinced myself that my body was good enough to be seen wearing only underwear in public by asking myself, "What would Virgie say?"), enjoying the water and sun, when I found myself (along with my friend who is half white/half Mexican, and white passing) in a very vulnerable and uncomfortable situation. We were talking to a seemingly nice young white couple, and their older, creepy white hippie friend, when the conversation turned racist. I spoke up and it got worse and we left. But this privilege, this ability to "dupe" the white gaze, if for a few minutes, coupled with the fact that I am also the kind of fat that leads well-meaning friends to say, "Stop. You're not fat," which almost feels a little bit like rejection (at least rejection of a part of myself), allows me to move a bit more freely across spaces than other fat folx. This fucked up privilege *allows* me to let the Mexican jump out, to be more myself, more "weird," more "quirky," more "different" without the same kind of repercussions (being silenced, omitted, rejected) because that light-skinned part of me has already been accepted. I can usually find clothes that fit in-store. Traveling is easy for me. Rarely is my weight pointed out in public. However, I have been given diet tips while on a date and, once, while out dancing with a fellow fat girl, a guy kept urging his girlfriend to "hit the fat girls." I had to remind my friend that we were educators and probably should keep our earrings on. For the most part, I do all right. And yet . . . sometimes I still don't feel enough.

Sometimes I'm still on survival mode. And when you're on survival mode, you don't have room for vulnerability, room to thrive, to grow.

> This dark hole
> I peer into
> pretends to be a mirror,
> pretends to be a truth-teller.
> Only sees one side of me
> and not even fully.
> But I remind myself,
> again and again,
> that looking into the mirror
> is like seeing an eclipse
> through a pinhole projector—
> you only see a semblance of the sun,
> a sliver of the wonder in the sky
> because its actual resplendence
> would surely blind you.

When I feel low, when the rolls feel extra, I look to women who inspire me. Women like Virgie Tovar, Yesika Salgado, and the first fat woman who let me see myself as enough: my friend Amanda. These women have showed me what it looks like when we love our bod-

ies. When we let ourselves be happy and live and thrive in our fat selves. They are vulnerable, they are real, and they are brave. Brave because this world doesn't like its women and femmes and nonbinary folx brave. Much less its fat women and fat femmes and fat nonbinary folx. Because if we're brave, if we love ourselves, if we say fuck your diet culture, fuck your beauty standards, fuck you, not only do we have time to devise different ways to bring down the patriarchy and create change, but we are seen as combative and promoting an unhealthy lifestyle. But how can one be considered healthy if we don't love our bodies? If worrying over calories or cheat days or diets causes anxiety? Makes us feel defeated? One thing I've learned from reading and following Virgie Tovar and other fat women on social media is how fat doesn't mean unhealthy, and thin doesn't equal healthy. There are so many things we ignore in those conversations— food deserts, access to health care, to mental health care, culture, physiology, heredity, poverty, personal choice. I do not deny that there are health issues that are related to being fat, but there are also health issues related to being thin. The difference is that one set of issues is always seen as more problematic and urgent.

I'm not here to tell you to stay fat, get fat, or not to lose weight. What I want to do is remind you that you own your body. Your body is yours. If you want to stay fat, stay fat. If you want to lose weight, lose weight. But remember that your body is worthy of love simply because it exists. I know that it's hard. But there is a freedom to wearing a crop trop and letting the panza out in a beautiful hot springs without caring what other people have to say. And people, well, they will always have something to say. Those people, they don't want you to thrive. To grow and own your power. Those people are concerned with staying in boxes that fit just so, and don't have the imagination or pleasure of knowing that beauty and love can be fat. They are cursed with being boring, with conformity, with fear. They are not concerned with your comfort, but with theirs.

And our job is not to exist to make other people comfortable or to convince them of our worth. Our job is to exist and thrive.

CHARLES LENIDA

ISABEL QUINTERO

is a writer and the daughter of Mexican immigrants. She lives and writes in the Inland Empire of Southern California. *Gabi, A Girl in Pieces*, her first YA novel, was the recipient of several awards, including the William C. Morris YA Debut Award. She's also the author of a chapter book series, Ugly Cat & Pablo; a nonfiction YA graphic biography, *Photographic: The Life of Graciela Iturbide*, which received the Boston Globe–Horn Book Award; and a picture book, *My Papi Has a Motorcycle*. Isabel also writes poetry and essays. Her work can be found in various print and online journals.

Can't Find Your Community? Create Your Own

by
BRUCE STURGELL

I didn't really find the place I fit in until I was thirty.

I realized I was a fat kid at a pretty young age. Schoolkids can be brutal; family members can be thoughtless with their comments. At the time, I felt like being fat meant that I was less than everyone else. That stayed with me, in many ways, until I was much older.

My childhood and teen years weren't horrible, but there was always this nagging voice in the back of my mind that told me that I wasn't good enough because of my size. Even with great friends and a loving family, I learned a terrible, false lesson that the mainstream world tries to teach us: Fat people don't deserve dignity.

I pushed that knowledge down deep inside and continued forward. I was funny, artistic, and loving. I made new friends and read comic books and drew constantly. I knew that I was fat, but that wasn't all there was to me. Thankfully, my parents reinforced this in their own ways. My mom taught me that being kind, loving, and optimistic is a good way to go through life. That forgiveness goes a long way and that you should love people for their differences, because those things make us great.

My dad taught me tenacity, stubbornness. He taught me never to give up on things I believed in and to look for creative solutions to problems. He also possessed a fiery independent streak, some of which he passed down to me. That trait in particular made me more self-reliant and less apt to ask for help. That independence eventually drove me to create the kind of community I was unable to find when I needed it most.

Even with all those things working in my favor, I couldn't shake the feelings of worthlessness that seemed to be floating right below the surface. I did my best not to let any of this show. Going through the world as a bigger kid is tough, and at times it felt like there was someone at every corner ready to share a nasty remark or laugh with their friends behind my back. In reality, those situations were few and far between, but they did happen. Maybe it was a random comment from a family member or a fat joke at my expense from someone I barely knew. When they

happened, they were devastating—and they stuck with me.

As I moved from my late teens into my early twenties, I started to get a grip on what (I thought) I wanted to do with my life. Radio! I started working for a small broadcasting company, first as in intern, then a DJ, then as marketing manager. I was working with amazing people, learning new things every day. Basically, living my dream. Even though my career was great, in my head, I was still that chubby kid who didn't measure up. I threw myself into my work. I had friends to hang out with and colleagues who respected me. But I still felt alone. So much of it was a feeling of alienation from people who weren't physically like me.

My career in radio ended, and I decided I needed to put on my big-boy pants (no pun intended) and find a real job. I took my experience in radio marketing and started helping companies with websites figure out how to get more customers. It was a less adventurous job than being a DJ, but it paid the bills, and I kept doing it for more than a decade.

When I started my marketing office job, there was a dress code. The problem was, I had no idea how to make that work. I had an ill-fitting dress shirt, some pants, and a tie I didn't know how to tie. I bought some polos and a few more pairs of pants and called it a day. But none of these clothes fit me well, so I didn't feel good in them. Unsure of what to do about that, I bought bigger, baggier clothes. It seemed like that was the only answer for big guys. But all this did was succeed in hiding me away while making me feel worse about myself. Your style is an extension of your personality. The clothes and accessories you wear can help show the world who you are in a way that you can't verbally convey. This is just one of the reasons that being able to find clothes in your size that you actually want to wear is so important.

In my teens, style was SO important to me! Yes, even fat teens, and even fat teen boys, care about style. Maybe you're one of them! I liked wild patterns, interesting fabrics, and bold clothes. Putting thought into my look helped me stand out. It was also one of the ways I pushed back against the idea that I was worth less if I was fat. I wanted people to know that I was funny, friendly, adventurous, and interesting. My clothes helped people understand me in a way that I couldn't always verbalize. Looking back, I see now that this is probably when I first started to realize that what other people think about you doesn't matter. How *you* feel about yourself does.

I came to this realization relatively early. In my experience—doing the work I do—this is kind of unique. I talk to a lot of guys who are significantly older and are just coming to that realization now. Part of it for me was the rebellious streak I got from my dad—he made it clear that being yourself and pushing back against systems and the status quo was positive.

During the radio years, the only clothing requirement was that you actually wear clothes. This meant I wore a lot of band T-shirts and baggy cargo shorts (don't laugh—it was the early 2000s! We all made mistakes!). Casual and functional was the name of the game. I stopped thinking about what I was wearing and how I felt in it. I was also getting bigger, and knowing that all I had to do was find a T-shirt in the next biggest size was easy and comforting, at least for a while.

When I was twenty-seven, I took a business trip to Washington, D.C. When we had some downtime, a coworker and I went to the White House, since I had never seen it. He took a photo of me at the front fence, and when I saw that photo for the first time, I hated what I saw. My shirt was too tight, and I was obviously uncomfortable. The person I saw in the photo wasn't who I wanted to be any longer. I didn't realize it at the time, but that moment is where the idea for Chubstr began.

When I got back from my trip, I knew I needed to find clothes I felt good about wearing. I was living in a smallish town in the Midwest where there weren't many options for men of any size, let alone a big and tall guy. Still, I wanted to see what I could find, so I headed to the local mall.

For plus-size people, the mall can be fraught with heartache and frustration. I learned this the hard way. I was at a size where sometimes, if I was lucky, I could find something that fit me. Usually, I would leave

Yes, even fat teens, and even fat teen boys, care about style.

empty-handed. When I walked into a shop, I could tell in the first thirty seconds how it was going to go. I would head to the back of the store, where the biggest sizes usually resided. If I couldn't find anything that fit me there, I would usually just leave. Sometimes, I would take a chance with an employee.

You've probably seen the look, right? When you walk into a store and the person behind the counter sees you and rolls their eyes. They know there's nothing there for you, and you know there's nothing there for you. They don't understand why you're even stopping in. Begrudgingly, they come over to help. The exchange usually ends with them saying that the shop doesn't carry your size. You leave, having gotten no real help and with no alternatives.

This was my life for a few years. Go to the mall, leave without purchasing anything. Try to go to the big-and-tall stores, only to find that the clothes they carried were made for my dad, not for me. Go home with nothing. Every time I did this, my frustration continued to build. I wasn't finding what I needed, and no one seemed to want to help me out. One day, after leaving the mall yet again with a whole lot of nothing, I decided to do something about it.

I went to the Internet to complain.

It was a spur-of-the-moment decision, starting a style blog. I had played around with personal blogs in the past. They were more of the online diary type, not really some-

thing for other people to read and respond to. Technically, when I started this newest blog, it wasn't really a style blog. It was a place for me to go to call out companies that weren't carrying clothes in extended sizes, or to complain about how difficult it was to find things I wanted online.

The site that would eventually become Chubstr was originally called Big Boy Fashion. If that doesn't tell you how little forethought I put into this, nothing else will. I started BBF on Tumblr, because I had seen how vibrant and interesting a community it was at that time. Whatever people were into, you could find it there. Women's plus-size fashion bloggers were really just starting to come into their own. I saw how unapologetically out there they were, and I loved it. From their amazing looks, to the way they talked about the intersection of fashion and body positivity, I was totally inspired. The problem was, nobody I could find was doing anything like that for men. I wanted to change that.

On Big Boy Fashion, I called out brands that could do better with their plus-size options, and I shared photos of my own looks. My posts would share resources, telling readers where I found the clothes I was wearing, so that they could buy them for themselves.

It was fun for me and it was a great way to share my feelings on being overlooked by an entire industry. To my surprise, people started to respond to what I was doing. They were liking my posts and sharing my photos. Better yet, they wanted advice on where to find things in their size, plus they shared their stories and pictures of their own looks that they loved! This was becoming something more important than simply a soapbox. There was a community.

The name Big Boy Fashion wasn't going to cut it. My experience in marketing told me that I could build something better. That's basically how Chubstr was born.

Chubstr's "official" mission statement is "To help people of size find, create, and share their style with the world." That's really just one part of it. At its core, Chubstr shows people that they deserve dignity regardless of their size. We do that not just through clothing, but also through interviews with bigger people living interesting lives, through stories about the experiences—good, bad, and ugly—that plus-size people have every day. We try to show the world what it is to be a bigger person in this day and age. That gives my writers and me a lot of area to cover.

Remember how I talked about what style meant to me when I was a teen? It made me feel stronger; it made me push back against all the crap out there that tells us that we're not good enough. I quickly realized that Chubstr could do the same thing for people. When you see a photo shoot up on the site, you're seeing photos of plus-size people living their best lives. You're seeing them in an inspirational light—looking great in clothes that fit them, or out in the world doing something amazing. We're not seeing things like this on TV, in movies, or in magazines, so I built something that offers what is missing.

The first time I realized that a community like Chubstr could make a difference was when I came across Jimbo Pellegrine. He was a pro surfer who happens to be a big guy. A photographer took photos of Jimbo in action: on his board in the middle of a wave, doing tricks, and just generally blowing minds. At that point, I didn't even know that it was possible for big guys to surf. I had been told that boards weren't big enough to hold guys my size, so seeing Jimbo on one changed everything.

I needed to talk to him, to interview him for Chubstr. I tracked him down through social media and reached out. Amazingly, he responded to me and was willing to chat. We talked about how he got started, how he pushed back against people's preconceived notions of what it means to be a bigger person, and how he had begun teaching other people to surf. He showed me that your size didn't have to be a limitation, like I had been told all my life.

When the article went up on the site along with the photos, the reaction was overwhelming. People loved the interview, and the photos inspired Chubstr readers just like they did me. This was the kind of thing we wanted to see but just weren't getting anywhere else. I knew that I was on the right track and that we needed more of this.

Since then, we've interviewed or featured actors, activists, an ACLU lawyer, designers, models, and writers. People who are doing great things in the world and who happen to be fat. When we interview these people, we don't always focus on their size. It's a thing, but it's not the *only* thing.

Chubstr has become more than a blog. We have a team of writers, have launched multiple video series, and even have a shop that offers a curated selection of clothing in sizes XL and up. The longer I do this, the more opportunities I see to offer our community the things that nobody else is doing for them. It's still amazing to me that this thing I started without much forethought has turned into something that not only helps me, but other people all over the world.

Creating Chubstr allowed me to find what I needed: people who shared my experiences and found the strength to keep moving forward. Every day I'm inspired by the messages we receive and by the people who get something from the work we're doing. I've met amazing people who helped me realize that my size has nothing to do with my value in the world, and that I'm as deserving of love and dignity as anyone else. Now I know I'm not alone or lesser, and that makes all the difference in the world.

Not seeing what you need out there in the world? You don't need to wait until you're thirty like I did—go ahead and build it for yourself! You don't have to create an expansive body positive community. Start smaller and focus on what matters to you. Create a blog or get on social media and join the conversation. Visit Chubstr or look up the work of the other creators in this book. Chances are, you'll be welcomed into the community and you'll make some new friends. Look for real-world experiences to connect with body positive events in your area. They're more common than you might think.

If you still can't find an existing group, you can harness the power of the Internet to start one of your own. Create a meet up or an event for plus-size teens that feels right for you. Don't worry if it takes a while to catch on. Great things can take time.

The bottom line is, your size doesn't dictate your worth. You deserve respect. You are awesome right now, today, as you are. Don't let anybody tell you different.

BRUCE STURGELL

is the founder of Chubstr.com, a fashion and lifestyle website for plus-size men. Chubstr.com helps people find, create, and share their masculine style with the world through articles, interviews, guides, and photo shoots featuring plus-size people. Get it all at the website or on Instagram @chubstr.

Your Journey to Being #fatandfree

by
SAUCYÉ WEST

I truly believe that our ideals of beauty are shaped and imprinted on us by the age of nine. That is when I started my period and my body started changing. I began to notice I was taller than the other boys and girls in my class. I even began to see who the boys thought were pretty. And I never was looked at in that way. By then we've absorbed what is acceptable and what is not acceptable. A lot of those ideals are taught to us by our parents or close family. Many of us are told that fat is bad and thin is beautiful. We then hear it again at school, through the lens of popularity. Why are the popular girls popular? I know I idolized certain people at school because they were beautiful, or they dressed well, or their hair was longer than mine. And yes, often because they were smaller.

I took my "I Don't Care" pill when I was fourteen. I was so exhausted with trying to fit into the parameters others had placed on my life. I was tired of existing in a world where I was constantly trying to please people. I had to make a choice. I had to look at myself and decide to love myself exactly the way I was. Now, this was not just a one-pill fix. I went to counseling and had the support of my close friends and eventually my family. And with those tools, I built a solid foundation for who I wanted to be.

This journey is not going to be easy. You are going to have to dig deep and really visualize yourself at a higher level. In life we often place emphasis on low-level tasks and procrastinate on larger issues, wondering all the while why we aren't seeing progress. This is certainly the way many people look at things in terms of bodies. You may think, "I don't like myself, so let me change." And then you realize that even after you change physically, you still aren't happy. It's because changing your hair or losing weight is not going to help with what is really going on inside you. Those things are not going to help you pave the way to really loving and accepting yourself—the key ingredients to happiness.

I want to give you some tools you can use to begin your road to self-love and acceptance. I want to help you deconstruct hurtful ideals and start this beautiful journey to taking back your freedom. Let's start with this exercise!

Things you will need: POST-ITS, MARKER.

I want you to write on Post-its all the things you do not like about yourself. Write everything you have been told was wrong about you, or traits you feel you need to change about yourself. Dig deep—the only person you are facing is yourself. If you need to cry or take breaks in between, that is fine. This is definitely a challenge, but you've got this!

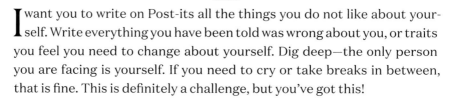

Place each Post-it on your bathroom mirror or on a wall in no particular order.

Now I want you to take down each Post-it that lists a trait someone *else* has told you was negative. Take down everything you were taught wasn't right about how you look. Rip down all the notes that represent societal norms and don't come from within you.

4

Take a look at what's left. Are most of those notes in the trash? I bet they are, because they are other people's thoughts. The fact is: We are born with confidence. Yes, I said it: We are born with confidence! Now that you have taken down other people's criticisms, you will be left with the actual issues you have to work on.

5

Study these remaining Post-its, work on them, and embrace them. And if they're based in fear, know that you can conquer anything by facing it head-on. Let the world know that you aren't afraid of loving yourself. Remember not to take these notes down until you truly feel that you have overcome them.

OK . . . so how am I supposed to do that? you may be wondering.

Remember when I said you create forward movement by visualizing yourself at a higher level? Also, things don't happen overnight. I am merely giving you a prescription for your own "I Don't Care" pill. Your pill might look different than mine, and it might take you longer to get there, but that's OK. This will be a process, just like everything else in life. It takes time to unlearn things that you have been taught.

The next step is to take those notes that are remaining and write down things you are going to do to change your self-narrative.

Let's look at some examples of what your notes might say:

My belly is too big.
I am scared to show my arms.
I'm just not confident.

Let's take *My belly is too big*. What are some things you can do to change that narrative? Why do you feel that way? What are some things you can do so that you can begin to love and embrace your belly? Here's an example of some things you might do to change this thought:

My belly is too big.

How will I learn to embrace my belly?

•

Look at inspiration on
social media every day.

•

Give my belly positive affirmations every day.

•

Buy a crop top and wear it
by the end of the month.

Bit by bit, this is how you create your road map for self-love. You are taking your issues and creating a goal for overcoming them. Then you are taking your time and being consistent and thoughtful in making sure your goal is met. You are examining your issue, creating a goal, and making sure you establish daily tasks to keep you on track. Remember: You can have more than three tasks to help you achieve this goal. You may have twenty! But you must hold yourself accountable, or you will continue to cling to these issues.

Your overall goal is to conquer your fears and tell society that *you* are the standard. The beautiful thing about creating a road map is that there is a final destination. And for those of us whose struggle is with our bodies, I'm here to tell you that there is an end to the struggle. Any time you feel you can't do it, or you won't get there, look at that map.

You are worthy, you are beautiful, and you are important. You have the right to live and love yourself in your fat body. The journey will be hard, and you will want to give up. But this is an exercise to show you how strong you are. Imagine how strong you will feel once you are able to take the last of those notes down, crumple it up, and throw it away.

I know you can do this. And I know you will be able to create your own road map to being #fatandfree.

SAUCYÉ WEST

is an African American freelance plus-size model, blogger, and body positive activist living in Sacramento, California. After feeling hesitation on whether to post a photo to Instagram or not, Saucye launched #FatAndFree, a body positive hashtag meant to encourage women from all backgrounds to love their bodies as they are, in this moment. Find her online @saucyewest.

Confidence

---

by
CORISSA ENNEKING

Be confident. That's what people tell us now. Fat people can be beautiful, you just have to be confident! Confidence is the new pretty. You can achieve anything as long as you're confident. But while we're being told this is the key to loving ourselves, we're being accosted with language and images that tell us otherwise:

Be confident in your body

* diet pill commercial plays on the radio! *

Love yourself

* the store you're in doesn't sell your size! *

Everyone is beautiful

* the thin model on TV says! *

How does anyone expect us to just wake up and be confident in a world that tells us every day *not* to be? And what exactly is this *confidence* thing everyone is talking about?

The problem with all the confidence rhetoric is that it doesn't give people a true picture of what confidence looks like or how it is gained. Confidence, by definition, is the belief in one's abilities. Now let's break down what that really looks like.

Confidence is not looking fly as hell on Instagram. It is not walking around with your head held high. It is not an aura that someone exudes. Confidence is the belief that you are capable.

When it's put that way, it becomes a bit clearer why people have such a hard time with it. Believing you are a capable human being can get fucked up pretty much anywhere along the way in your life. And once it's fucked up, it's pretty hard to fix it. Let's quit talking about confidence as your goal. Feeling confident and believing you are capable become easier as you make your way toward loving yourself. The goal is not confidence; the goal is to love ourselves wholly and completely. Because when that happens, confidence will come naturally.

First and foremost, we have to speak kindly to ourselves. When my best friend's son was about two, he went through a mild rebellious phase, and my best friend bore the brunt of that phase. We all know that children mean no harm and it takes them some time to learn boundaries, but it was still painful for my friend. One day he said something hurtful to her, and I saw tears well up in her eyes. Before I could catch myself, I looked right at him and said, "Don't talk to my friend like that!" He looked a bit shocked and proceeded to apologize to his mom. I couldn't believe I just said that to a two-year-old. He didn't know his words had that kind of impact! Well, that voice inside your head doesn't know its impact, either. That voice inside your head has been hearing and speaking cruel things for as long as it can remember, and you're going to have to set some boundaries with it. Now when I have a negative thought about myself, I say to that voice in my head, "Don't talk to my friend like that!" It doesn't always stop the nasty thoughts, but it almost always slows them down . . . and makes me giggle a little bit.

Once you slow down your thoughts, you've got to start doing a little fact-checking.

What exactly is this *confidence* thing everyone is talking about?

It turns out we're told a lot of bullshit for a lot of years, so you've got to start asking yourself, "Why the hell do I think that?" If you see your thighs in the mirror and think they have too much cellulite, try asking yourself, "Why do I think that? What constitutes *too much* anyway?" Is there a scale on which you're measuring the amount of cellulite on your legs? Or do you think there's too much cellulite on your thighs because some kid made a joke about cottage cheese legs when you were fifteen? Does that kid get to decide how you feel about your body forever after? No way!

It's important to remember that sometimes we find out someone we really care about may be one of the sources of bad thoughts we have about our bodies. It's OK to be upset about that, and it's OK to address it with that person. There's no need for it to hold you back, though. You do not have to resolve every issue with everyone who ever hurt you before you love yourself.

Lastly, stop judging others. Here's the thing: You don't need to stop judging others for some greater good or because it's nice. You've got to do it because every time you judge someone, you store that judgment in a little vault. And on your worst days, you un-lock that vault and you let those judgments pour out onto yourself. Practicing love and non-judgment for others is a great way to build self-love. Sometimes we might think we are judging people because we care about them. Judging someone and masking it as "concern" is condescending and unnecessary. Unsolicited advice is never good advice. You are not more informed on another person's life than they are. Once you slow down your judgments of others, your judgments of yourself will naturally follow suit.

So that's it! You're magically going to love yourself now, right? Well, not exactly. You've got to remember that society has been planting these hurtful ideas in our heads for our whole lives. It's going to take a little bit of time to unlearn them and start accepting ourselves. You'll need to practice and be gentle with yourself when you fail. It won't be easy, and in fact, sometimes it will be hard. That's OK. You can cope with difficult. You are capable of unlearning the lies you've been taught. You *are* capable. You are so incredibly capable.

And that's where we gain confidence: in the experience of unlearning what we've been taught and finding our truest selves. It's a wild ride, but it is so incredibly worth it.

You're worth it.

CORISSA ENNEKING

is a fat activist and body positive blogger at FatGirlFlow.com. She has a major obsession with plants, bikinis, and summertime. Her activism focuses on providing resources for plus-size shoppers about where to purchase clothing that will fit them and make them feel incredible. You can find Corissa on Instagram @fatgirlflow and on Twitter @fatgirlfreedom.

Make Your Own Self-Care Kit

By Rachelle Abellar

Existing as a fat person in this world is not easy, and the journey to fat acceptance and liberation can be a tough one to navigate. This is why self-care is vital to our survival. All bodies are valuable and deserve to be prioritized and cared for.

Keeping a self-care kit at the ready can prove extremely useful in times of need. Having many tools in one place makes it easier to deal with your feelings in a safe and healthy way instead of reverting to negative or self-destructive behaviors. What you fill your kit with is up to you, but here are some ideas to get you started!

a container to put everything in

letters & notes

fidget toys

your favorite snack

PEACH GUMMIES

a journal or sketchbook

art supplies

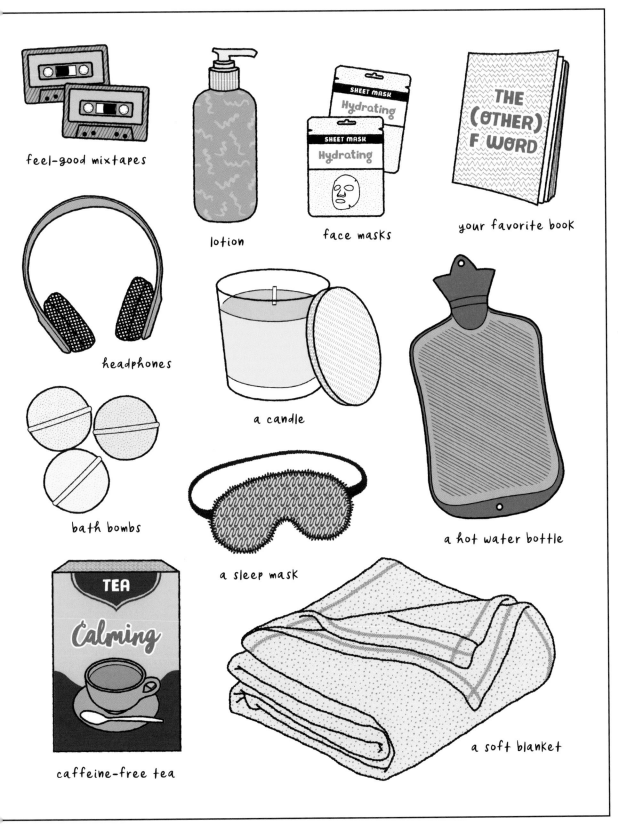

feel-good mixtapes

lotion

face masks

your favorite book

THE (OTHER) F WORD

SHEET MASK
Hydrating

SHEET MASK
Hydrating

headphones

a candle

a hot water bottle

bath bombs

a sleep mask

TEA
Calming

caffeine-free tea

a soft blanket

RACHELLE ABELLAR

is a graphic designer, fat activist, and body liberation advocate. She is the founder of PNW Fattitude, a group that hosts events for people of size in the Pacific Northwest. She is best known for her self-care zines, as well as *The Little Book of Big Babes*, a coffee-table book documenting fat fashion all over the world. When she's not busy making zines, Rachelle spends a lot of time drinking bubble tea and thinking about the intersection of fatness and fandom. You can find her on most social media @rachelleabellar.

Losing My Religion

by
JESS WALTON

The first time I joined Weight Watchers, I was in high school.

I felt all grown up;

I had been accepted into the church of weight loss,

adult women praying together that their numbers have
gone down,

cheering as parts of them fell away,

each hated kilo of their bodies offered up to their god.

They had their saints, too, so familiar to a Catholic girl like me:

women who had made it, reached their goal weight.

Thinner, better versions of themselves somehow,

and never going back to hell,

to that place where fat women live,

stared at and judged and joked about,

seen as lesser than because they are more than

the weight that patriarchy finds acceptable, desirable,
fuckable.

I did the program, I followed the rules,

I counted the points, I went to the meetings . . .

I weighed myself over and over and over again.

Eventually I learned that I can lose twelve kilos and still hate my
body,

still feel *too fat*.

I can lose twelve kilos and still need to lose more, more, more

because this church is a cult, and their gospel is self-loathing,

and if I were named a saint,

graced the pages of their magazines,

I would spend my life desperate to stop those numbers creeping
back up,

fighting temptation, confessing my sins, and weighing my worth.

I wondered what would happen if I stopped

hating and hurting myself, and instead

worked on loving myself;

worked on *being* myself instead of *becoming* myself,

and maybe even letting others love me

as I am?

What if

I was just

fat?

What would it be like

if my before photo was the same as my after photo?

Fat then, fat now;

the only difference the smile on my happy, fat face.

Amazing! What a transformation!

A beautiful fat, queer, disabled girl,

living my best life,

achieving my *real* goals.

The *last* time I joined Weight Watchers,

I knew, deep down, it was over.

I went to a meeting, rows of beautiful people

watching and weighing and praying and waiting

and fervently hating themselves.

No.

Now no gaze can touch me, no patriarchy shame me,

and no cult will turn my mind against my body, ever again.

Let them look at me and think that I have failed.

I know in my heart that I have already won this game.

No scales can get the measure of who I am.

My body is a part of me,

and I will love it all.

I will run my hand over voluptuous rolls of fat,

meeting each other and hiding my belly button,

making secrets in my flesh.

My body is a landscape, its features and contours

are mine, and mine alone.

I will run my hand over silvery lines that streak across my thighs, nothing stretched about them.

They have just grown with me as I grew:

proof that I am here, and my body is real,

and my life and the world have made marks

on my skin, that papyrus of organs,

that teller of tales.

I will run my hand over scars where surgeons cut deep,

the one on my left leg the longest.

Thin and red, it curves up at the ends like a smile.

Tracing it with a finger, I feel my ghost limb roar into furious life,

tingling and tickling beyond the boundaries of my body.

My body is a book full of poems,

every inch a story

about who I am,

and where I have been,

and where I might go from here.

JESS WALTON

is a fat, queer, disabled writer and teacher from Melbourne, Australia. She is the author of *Introducing Teddy*, a picture book about a transgender teddy bear. In 2017 Jess completed a Write-ability Fellowship with Writers Victoria, focused on short stories and poetry about disability, cancer, and pain. In 2018 she wrote "Stars in Our Eyes," a short story about a queer, disabled teenager for YA anthology *Meet Me at the Intersection*. Jess recently cowrote an episode of the Australian comedy TV show *Get Krack!n*; the episode, focused on disability, aired in 2019.

You Are Loved

by
ADY DEL VALLE

Fashion and style are how many of us choose to express ourselves to the world regardless of our size. Society has put fat people in a box for years and has tried to dictate how we should dress or express ourselves. But the truth is, fashion has no size, fashion doesn't discriminate, and fashion doesn't tell you how you should look. Style is how you choose to represent yourself to the world. Being fat and loving fashion is part of who I am; it's also a form of self-care for me. Wearing pieces that make me feel good and confident helps me to walk with my head held high because I feel fabulous in what I am wearing, and I can express that with my vibe and presence—no words necessary.

You should feel confident and amazing about yourself whether or not you make an effort to keep up with fashion. Fashion is just an accessory for who we already are. In a world where we are told, "NO, you can't wear that" or "You can't be that," because you're fat—that's where you create your own path. In your own, self-made world you can say, "YES, I can wear that and be that." That's something I live and practice every day.

As fat people, we will always have obstacles that will threaten to topple our self-esteem. It's OK to have down days—we are all human. But never allow the occasional challenge to take over your life or keep you down. Lift yourself up. Surround yourself with positive people who love you as you are and help enhance the person you are. Every day tell yourself something positive about yourself. Put on the cute piece that makes you look and feel fabulous when you step out.

Wearing the largest size as a plus-size male model hasn't been an easy road. People have told me, "You're too fat," or, "You're shooting too high at stars that aren't there," because that's what society has dictated. We have been constantly told we aren't worthy of being represented in the industry, or we shouldn't pursue certain dreams.

Not only am I the biggest in size currently active in the modeling industry, but I am also gay and Latino. I represent a vast audience that struggles in society overall. This is why I have never given up and will never give up: because I want to be what I never *had*. I want to be that representation you see and can relate to when you flip the pages of a magazine or the channels on TV.

I want you to see yourself in me and say: "I want to be that or do that!" Because you can. Fashion modeling is the platform I have embraced to show the world that we as fat people are worthy and capable as we are, no changes needed. I've tried to pave the way for anyone following in my footsteps in the modeling industry.

Remember: You can be fat, but you're still beautiful, worthy, wanted, and fabulous. *Fat* isn't a bad word. Being fat is a part of who we are, but it doesn't limit who we can become.

You are loved.

ADY DEL VALLE

is a big-and-tall male model. He is also a body positive and LGBTQ advocate. Ady is the first plus-size male model to be featured in an editorial fashion magazine. He is very passionate about inclusivity in fashion and media for people of all sizes, ages, genders, and disabilities. You can learn and find more about Ady on his social media accounts via Instagram @Adydelvalle_ or Facebook @Ady Del Valle.

Fat Acceptance Is (Really) Real

by
EVETTE DIONNE

How old were you when you first realized it's wrong to be racist? If you were educated in public schools—as I was—it was around the age of eight, when your third-grade teacher offered a two- or three-week lesson during Black History Month about the civil rights movement. Often it's a truncated recap that focuses on four key moments: Black people in the South (only in the South, though the North was full of racism, too) were forced to use segregated facilities, including public restrooms, buses and trains, and water fountains; Rosa Parks, an elderly seamstress who was tired after a long day of work, refused to relinquish her bus seat to a white patron, and her arrest sparked the Montgomery Bus Boycott; Martin Luther King Jr. made a galvanizing speech in 1963 in Washington, D.C., that encouraged President Lyndon B. Johnson to sign the Civil Rights Act of 1964; and then racism ended, and being racist turned previously powerful people into social pariahs. Not only does this revisionist history overlook all the work that organizers and demonstrators—including Parks—did to force the United States to reckon with its mistreatment of people of color, but it also erases all the violence inflicted on people of color and Black people before the Voting Rights Act and all the violence that people of color and Black people still experience.

Yet, these fluffy academic lessons serve their purpose: Children learn that discriminating against someone based on their ethnicity is unacceptable, and those who are overtly racist can face social and legal consequences, including losing their jobs, being shunned in their communities, and even being imprisoned if their hatred fuels a violent act. As we've seen in a recent string of viral videos that feature white people harassing people of color for doing mundane activities, such as selling lemonade, barbecuing in parks, and using a valid coupon in a convenience store, in-your-face racism often comes with a steep cost. In our society, however, similar penalties aren't levied against those who discriminate against fat people. In fact, maligning fat people is still considered socially acceptable. Think about it: Have you ever attempted to insult someone by calling them fat? How often do you see plus-size people on television who aren't on weight-loss shows like *My 600-lb Life* or *The Biggest Loser*? Are you or any of your friends currently dieting, talking about dieting, or watching commercials that encourage dieting?

More than likely, you'll be saying yes to at least one, if not all, of these questions—because fat shaming is stitched into the fabric of American culture. In fact, it's so embedded in our everyday lives that we don't often recognize when we're perpetuating fatphobia, or the act of discriminating against someone because of the size of their body. For instance,

Michigan is the only state that has passed a law that forbids employers from penalizing fat people in the workplace, which means that in forty-nine states, people of size can be fired, denied promotions, and paid less than their straight-size counterparts.[1] While children are often taught to use the Golden Rule to guide their interactions with all people, especially those who are different than they, unfortunately, treating others as we'd like to be treated isn't considered when legislators are passing the laws that govern our lives. We can see how that lack of regulation leads to discrimination: Fat applicants are less likely to be hired than straight-size applicants because hiring managers tend to associate fatness with laziness, according to a 2017 survey conducted by Fairygodboss.[2] We can also see it in the fact that fat employees earn $1.25 less per hour[3] than straight-size employees, which can lead to a loss of $100,000 over the course of a career.

Fatphobia doesn't just appear in the workplace, either. In 2003, researchers found that more than 50 percent of the primary-care physicians they surveyed viewed obese patients as "awkward, unattractive, ugly, and noncompliant," and the majority of these doctors "view obesity as largely a behavioral problem and share our broader society's negative stereotypes about the personal attributes of obese persons."[4] While we know that fat people are stigmatized in every area of their lives, it holds a different weight

"We want to show
we feel happy, not
guilty. That's why
we're here."

when doctors—not fashion designers or magazine editors—have a negative view of people of size. Dr. Lilia Graue told Healthline that doctors often "fail to provide adequate and timely diagnosis and treatment due to all kinds of assumptions, [which] affects patients along the full weight spectrum."[5] These biases can have a deadly impact on fat people: Patients of size are less likely to seek medical care because they're afraid of being fat shamed by their doctors. This in turn can lead to diseases, such as ovarian cancer, being caught later and in more advanced stages. It can also result in fat patients being misdiagnosed, as writer Rebecca Hiles explained in *Cosmopolitan* in April 2018. For five years, she experienced coughing fits that caused her to have spasms and rely on adult diapers. Doctors told her that losing weight would alleviate her symptoms, but after a coughing fit landed her in the emergency room, she learned that she had a tumor in a bronchial tube. Her entire left lung had to be removed.[6]

No matter where fat people go—schools, workplaces, and courtrooms—we face being ostracized and discriminated against, and that's the reason why fat acceptance activists have been fighting since the 1960s to make America's policies more inclusive of people of size. As Sarai Walker, author of *Dietland*, told

Refinery29 in 2016, fat acceptance is believing that "bodies come in all shapes and sizes, and that all bodies have equal value. Fat activism is a political movement that advocates for the rights and dignity of fat people," she concluded.[7]

Just as the civil rights movement has an extensive history that exceeds what we're taught in school, the fat-acceptance movement has tangible roots that we should all be learning. It all began in 1967 when WBAI radio personality Steve Post decided to host a "fat-in" in Central Park because he, as a 210-pound man, faced size discrimination and he wanted to "protest discrimination against [fat people]." While there has been some debate about Post's intention for organizing a fat-in, what's clear is that it was the first event of its kind. "We want to show we feel happy, not guilty. That's why we're here," Post told the *New York Times* at the time.[8] This opened the door for more radical activism that focused intensely on making the world more equitable for fat people.

During this time, activists were focused on an array of social issues, including the Vietnam War, sexism, and racism, so the fight to end sizeism didn't gain the national attention it deserved, but that didn't stop fat-acceptance activists from bringing awareness. While it seemed that fatphobia wouldn't be as big of a priority as ending an international war or upending segregation, the social and political climate provided fertile ground for all marginalized people, including fat people, to fight for equality. Two years after the Central Park fat-in, writer Llewelyn Louderback and activist Bill Fabrey formed the National Association to Advance Fat Acceptance (NAAFA) with the goal of ending fatphobic messages in media and making the world safer for people of size. For the past fifty years, NAAFA has lobbied for legislation, staged plus-size fashion shows, called out media organizations that offer fatphobic advertising and messaging, and worked to fulfill its mission, especially as more and more Americans gain weight.[9] (It's more important than ever to have laws that protect people of size from discrimination because seven in ten Americans are now classified as "overweight."[10])

Fat-acceptance activists were also integral in getting Michigan to pass that size-discrimination law, forcing the fashion industry to be more inclusive of different bodies, and taking on the billion-dollar dieting industry that often tells people that they're flawed and that their products can make them perfect. For instance, in 1993, Bonnie Cook sued the Ladd Center, a facility for people with disabilities in Rhode Island, for discriminating against her in the hiring process.[11] She claimed their refusal to rehire her because of her weight violated the Re-

habilitation Act of 1973, a law that is usually used to prove discrimination against people with disabilities. She was awarded $100,000 in damages, and the Ladd Center was ordered to hire her. It was a major victory for fat activists, who were lobbying for legislation to protect fat people from weight-based discrimination. That paved the way for Michigan's law and shifted how employers treated fat people.

Fat-acceptance activists and bloggers have also worked extensively to make the fashion industry more inclusive of different bodies, including transgender and disabled bodies. While fashion has long been an exclusive industry that caters to thin, white women, in the last several years designers, modeling agencies, and fashion magazines have begun offering more opportunities to underrepresented communities. During New York Fashion Week's Spring 2019 showings, forty-nine plus-size models walked in twelve shows, which is a vast improvement from the twenty-seven models of size who walked in Fall 2018's shows and the thirty-four who walked in NYFW's Spring 2018 presentations.[12] Plus-size models, including Ashley Graham and Tess Holliday, are also appearing on magazine covers and in fashion campaigns, and Graham even received her own Barbie in 2016. Yet, the goals of fat acceptance are still misunderstood.

In every way, fat acceptance is a movement designed to promote dignity so that people of size have equal access to opportunities. Despite this clear definition, fat acceptance is woefully misunderstood. This is best exemplified in an April 2018 column published in the *Guardian* by writer Lizzie Cernik. "Fronted by plus-sized models and social media influencers, the fat acceptance movement aims to normalize obesity, letting everyone know that it's fine to be fat," Cernik writes. "With terms such as 'straight size' and 'fat pride' proliferating, some influential figures are now even likening the valid concerns of health officials to hate crimes."[13] "Glorifying obesity" is a common misconception associated with fat acceptance. Asking for equality is not the same as "glorifying obesity," as writer Rachelle Hampton explains in a scathing rebuke published in Slate:

> Of course, fat people aren't trying to encourage more people to become fat; they're trying to live a life with dignity. If you've never been fat, it's hard to understand the various ways in which your body stops becoming your own once you reach a certain weight. It becomes an object for public consumption and comment or ridicule. Strangers feel obligated to tell you you're going to die early or give diet tips or scrutinize your every meal under the guise of patronizing concern for your health.[14]

Fat-acceptance activists also want a world where people of size are on-screen in narratives that don't center on their weight. A study conducted by Dr. Stacy L. Smith and the Media, Diversity & Social Change Initiative at USC Annenberg for Refinery29 found that of the top one hundred films released in 2016, only two women larger than a size fourteen were cast as a lead or a colead. Of the top fifty TV shows in 2016, 43 percent of women characters were thin, and only three women leads were larger than a size fourteen.[15] In a country where 67 percent of women are considered plus-size, but that majority only represents 2 percent of images,[16] it's crucial to have a movement that promotes fat inclusion and acceptance. When fat people are unable to see themselves on-screen and straight-size people never see fat people on-screen, it fuels the idea that only thin people are deserving of representation. That has a lingering impact on self-esteem and, of course, trickles down into how we interact with fat people in our lives.

Fat-acceptance activists envision a world where children aren't bullied because of the size of their bodies. In 2010, researchers at the University of Michigan released startling findings about how size intersects with childhood bullying. The researchers followed eight hundred children in ten cities across the United States and surveyed them, their teachers, and their mothers about the children's experience with bullying. They found that "kids who were obese were 65 percent more likely to be bullied than their peers of normal weight; overweight kids were 13 percent more likely to be bullied."[17] In order to create an equitable world for plus-size people, it has to begin in childhood, and that requires a confronting of how plus-size children are maligned because of their size.

Nowhere are these objectives rooted in "glorifying obesity." Instead, fat-acceptance activists want a different world where fat people can work, have relationships, be on-screen, grow up safely, and simply exist without facing discrimination. I've been considered overweight since I was eight, and unfortunately, I was surrounded by people who encouraged me to lose weight in order to gain dignity and respect. The idea that I was worth less because of the size of my body seeped into every area of my life; I didn't wear a swimsuit on a beach until I was twenty. It wasn't until I was twenty-two, in graduate school, and scouring the Internet, that I stumbled on communities of fat-acceptance bloggers and activists who'd developed better relationships with their bodies and were fighting for a more equitable world. You, dear teen reader, shouldn't have to wait that long. You can become involved in the fat-acceptance movement right now, and it really starts with you.

It's imperative that you find your voice and wield it as loudly as possible. If you think you're being discriminated against because of your size, call it out. If you see your friends speaking negatively about someone's body because it's larger than theirs, call them out. A simple, "That wasn't kind. You shouldn't talk about other people's bodies in that way," will suffice. If you go to the doctor for a sore throat, and the doctor immediately tries to weigh you, don't be afraid to tell them you're uninterested in being weighed or knowing your weight at this time. And most important, find friends who believe as you do—all bodies are good bodies, no matter their size, their shape, their ability, their ethnicity, or their gender. There is nothing wrong with wanting to be affirmed by people who understand how crucial it is to love your body as it is. In fact, there's an entire history of people who've done exactly that and fought for the dignity of fat people. You can learn that history and then carry on that legacy. In fact, the movement has been waiting for you all along.

If you're still unsure where to start, here's what I'd suggest: Author and fat-acceptance blogger Jes Baker has a list of 135 Instagram accounts you can follow that will diversify your feed and give you access to different bodies.[18] Her blog, *The Militant Baker*, also has a treasure trove of resources about fat acceptance, including books that people who are new to the movement can read. There are also organizations, like the National Association to Advance Fat Acceptance, the Council on Weight and Size Discrimination, and the Body Positive, that offer tool kits and in-person meet ups for those who want to learn more about fat acceptance. If you want to know about specific businesses and establishments that are accommodating to people of size, check out AllGo and Ample. And, of course, we're in the age of the podcast, so if you want to learn more about fat acceptance from a variety of people at different stages of their own journey, you should definitely listen to *She's All Fat*, *The Fat Lip*, the *Food Psych Podcast*, or *Fat Club Podcast*.

Just as we know that racism is wrong, we have to begin to understand and grasp that sizeism is wrong. It is harmful. It should come with a social consequence. And until that happens, we'll be here, and fighting, and wanting better. That's what fat acceptance is all about.

NOTES

1. Rebecca Puhl, Janet D. Latner, Kerry S. O'Brien, Joerg Luedicke, Sigrun Danielsdottir, and Ximena Ramos Salas, "**Potential Policies and Laws to Prohibit Weight Discrimination: Public Views from 4 Countries,**" *The Milbank Quarterly*, 93(4), 691–731.

2. Fairygodboss, "**The Grim Reality of Being a Female Job Seeker: If You're Overweight, Not 'Nice'-Looking, Older, or a Minority, You Won't Be Hired,**" 2017, bit.ly/2WMgf6r.

3. Charles L. Baum II and William F. Ford, "**The Wage Effects of Obesity: A Longitudinal Study,**" *Health Economics*, 13, no. 9 (September 2004), 885–899.

4. Gary D. Foster, Thomas A. Wadden, Angela P. Makris, Duncan Davidson, Rebecca Swain Sanderson, David B. Allison, and Amy Kessler, "**Primary Care Physicians' Attitudes about Obesity and Its Treatment,**" *Obesity*, 11, no. 10 (October 2003), 1168–1177.

5. Marie Southard Ospina, "**My Doctor Fat-Shamed Me— And I'm Not the Only One,**" Healthline, March 9, 2018, healthline.com/health-news/my-doctor-fat-shamed -me#1.

6. Maya Dusenbery, "**Doctors Told Her She Was Just Fat. She Actually Had Cancer,**" *Cosmopolitan*, April 17, 2018, cosmopolitan.com/health-fitness/a19608429 /medical-fatshaming/.

7. Kelsey Miller, "**What the Fat-Acceptance Movement Is Really About,**" Refinery29, July 25, 2016, refinery29 .com/en-us/2016/07/117556/fat-acceptance-movement -sizeism-explained.

8. "**Curves Have Their Day in Park; 500 at a 'Fat-in' Call for Obesity,**" *New York Times*, June 5, 1967, nytimes .com/1967/06/05/archives/curves-have-their-day-in -park-500-at-a-fatin-call-for-obesity.html.

9. Dan Fletcher, "**The Fat-Acceptance Movement,**" *Time*, July 31, 2009, content.time.com/time/nation /article/0,8599,1913858,00.html.

10. Christopher Ingraham, "**Nearly Half of America's Overweight People Don't Realize They're Overweight,**" *Washington Post*, December 1, 2016, washingtonpost.com/news/wonk/wp/2016/12/01 /nearly-half-of-americas-overweight-people-dont -realize-theyre-overweight/?noredirect=on&utm_term =.a9d809127ff3.

11. David P. Twomey, *Labor & Employment Law: Text and Cases* (Mason, Ohio: South-Western Cengage Learning, 2010).

12. Cordelia Tai, "**Report: Racial, Size, Gender and Age Diversity Reach All-Time High at New York Fashion Week Spring 2019,**" Fashion Spot, September, 25, 2018, thefashionspot.com/runway-news/805025-diversity -report-new-york-fashion-week-spring-2019/.

13. Lizzie Cernik, "**It's Not Fine to Be Fat. Celebrating Obesity Is Irresponsible,**" *Guardian*, April 10, 2018, theguardian.com/commentisfree/2018/apr/10/fat -pride-obesity-public-health-warnings-dangerous -weight-levels.

14. Rachelle Hampton, "**The Fat Pride Movement Promotes Dignity, Not a 'Lifestyle,'**" Slate, April 11, 2018, slate.com/human-interest/2018/04/fat-pride -movement-is-for-dignity-not-recruitment.html.

15. Anne Cohen, "**How Much Progress Has Hollywood Actually Made in Showing Body Diversity?,**" Refinery29, October 25, 2017, refinery29.com/en -us/2017/10/173864/plus-size-actresses-tv-movies-body -types-women.

16. Kelsey Miller, "**We Let You Down and We're Going To Fix It,**" Refinery29, September 26, 2016, refinery29 .com/en-us/2016/09/123687/plus-size-american-women -67-percent-essay.

17. Anne Harding, "**Obese Kids More Vulnerable to Bullies,**" CNN, May 3, 2010, cnn.com/2010 /HEALTH/05/03/obesity.bullying.index.html.

18. Jes Baker, "**135 Ways to Diversify Your Instagram Feed,**" *The Militant Baker*, May 4, 2107, themilitantbaker.com/2017/04/diversify-your- instagram-feed.html.

EVETTE DIONNE

is the editor in chief of Bitch Media, the author of the forth-coming books *Fat Girls Deserve Fairytales Too* and *Lifting As We Climb*, and a proud member of the Beyhive. You can find her work and her rantings about feminism online at @freeblackgirl.

50 Tips from a Fat and Fabulous Elder

by
MIGUEL M. MORALES

1. Support fat people.

2. That means you, too. Give yourself the same support you give others.

3. Don't let anyone make you feel like you have to hide food.

4. Always. Share. Your. Snacks.

5. No matter how fat you think you are, someone wishes they were as thin as you. You are their ideal weight. You inspire someone simply by existing.

6. Don't delete pictures or videos just because they make you look fat. Put them in a folder or tuck them away. Revisit them in time to see how your perspective changes.

7. You are the same beautiful person IRL that you are in your profile pic.

8. Every so often, take the middle seat. Let people navigate around you for once.

9. Refuse to be reseated for another person's comfort.

10. There's nothing wrong with failing; it doesn't mean you're a failure.

11. Kill diets. Kill all the diets.

12. Learn how to cook your mom's food.

13. Leave the house. Go outside. Be visible. People need to see us. They need to see our fat bodies out in the world. And we need to see each other.

14. If you find a pair of shoes you like, buy an extra pair. Shoes for fat feet are hard to find.

15. Wearing black is fine, but if you love color and patterns, wear them.

16. The purpose of a belt is to hold up your pants, not to measure your self-worth.

17. Drink lots of water.

18. Help an old fat person.

19. Ask for a bigger chair, a bigger bed, a bigger booth, or a bigger anything if you need it.

20. Don't let your size keep you from going to the water park or the festival or the concert or from volunteering to help others or from anything you want to do.

21. Finish school whether it's in person, online, or whatever is available.

22. There's at least one thing you can do better than anyone. Be proud of it. Protect it but never hide it.

23. You are sexy. You are sexual.

24. Being fat doesn't mean you're an object for another person's pleasure.

25. You can do better than that jerk.

26. "No" is an answer that doesn't require an explanation.

27. Trying to buy your way into someone's heart with gifts and favors will only make them want those things more and you less.

28. Sometimes walking away is all that you can do.

29. Just because someone likes you doesn't mean you have to like them back.

30. It's OK to get angry. Anger is a tool, like a hammer. It can be used to build or to destroy.

31. Sometimes things need to be destroyed before they can be rebuilt. It's scary but necessary. It's also beautiful. Respect it.

32. Take the last slice of pizza.

33. You are the same enchanting person that you sound like on the phone.

34. I cannot lie. Everyone likes big butts.

35. Sodium. Watch your sodium intake.

36. No one knows your body better than you. Not your parents. Not your siblings. Not your partner. Not your friends. Not your doctor. Not your dentist. Not your teacher. Not your pastor. No one.

37. Remember: No one fat shames trees or elephants for having junk in their trunks.

38. Be an ally to other marginalized people.

39. You are intersectional. Embrace all your identities—
    even the ones not apparent to others.

40. Go swimming without wearing a T-shirt.

41. If you like dancing or skiing or swimming or any kind
    of physical activity, do it without shame. People will
    always be watching. Some will watch to see your fail.
    Some will watch to see you succeed. Some will watch to
    assess your skill. Whatever the reason, amaze them.

42. Laugh but not at people's pain. Be sassy but not cruel.

43. Ask for help when you need it; offer help when it's
    needed.

44. Don't let anyone misgender you because of your
    fatness, whether it's by mistake or purposely. Make
    them call you who you are.

45. Carry a handkerchief with you. No one wants to be that
    fat, sweaty, hot mess in public.

46. Be open to giving and receiving love and friendship
    from people of all colors, shapes, sizes, and abilities.

47. You *do* have a pretty face (and the rest of you is also
    pretty).

48. Tell your story.

49. Share this book with someone so they can find
    themselves in it like you have.

50. Make this list fatter by adding your own tips.

Does this poem make me look fat?

by
MIGUEL M. MORALES

Does it mold around my torso
like a favorite tight-fitting shirt
offering glimpses of my underbelly
when I gesture, laugh, and flirt?

Does it cling to my tetas
drawing away your eye
from the creaminess and warmth
of my thick Latinx thighs?

Does it pour over me like water
rolling over rolls,
filling every crevice,
that you're desperate to behold?

Does it free you from the shaming
thoughts that you have formed
regulating our bodies
by imposing restrictive norms?

Does it start a revolution
right now where you are at?
By embracing your own fat body
and the calories you combat?

Does it offer a restful welcome
for you to stay and have a chat?
I ask, smiling with anticipation,
"Does this poem make me look fat?"

Elephant, Hippo, and Other Nicknames I Love

by
JES BAKER

Here comes Jes the Hippo!" someone sang loudly as I pulled open Mrs. Olsen's classroom door and entered. This trilling announcement of my arrival was loud enough to cause my entire fifth-grade class to turn toward me as I slid into my wooden desk seat.

I looked around for the owner of the singsong voice; my eyes eventually landed on a small girl grinning victoriously in my direction. Her name was Danielle, and if my life were to be told in comic-book form, she would undoubtedly make an appearance as my very first archnemesis.

I was a chubby, blond, prepubescent student; never part of the "cool crowd" thanks to (1) my uncontrollable desire to raise my hand and answer the question before anyone else *in addition to* (2) wearing the same orange socks purchased for me by my mom every week—I was completely unaware that, even for a youngster in the nineties, orange socks were apparently an *unforgivable* fashion choice. The semiaquatic mammalian nickname that stuck to me like glue for the rest of the year was simply the icing on my personal "Forever a Playground Loser" cake.

If I'm being completely honest, in the beginning I was fairly confident that this nickname was a compliment. While only having a short decade of life under my belt, I was nonetheless well aware that hippos—while seemingly whimsical—were not creatures to be messed with. I had watched enough National Geographic videos to know that hippos were capable of opening their jaws a full 150 degrees (Fun Fact: Their jaws can stretch to 4–5 feet wide) and could effortlessly crush a human skull. Even other keystone predators that surrounded them—like the formidably ruthless lion (who, by comparison, is only able to stretch its jaws to a paltry 11 inches)— were afraid of them. As far as I was concerned, hippos were to be revered and respected . . . or at least that's what I thought until I heard other students whispering about our classmate Helen "the Elephant" as well. The scathing tone used to describe her resemblance to this *other* (in my opinion) magnificent creature was my first red flag that being compared to an enormous mammal wasn't something I was meant to feel flattered by.

It took me mere days to realize that Helen and I were not being compared to animals because of our impressive capacity for memory or monumental jaw strength. Quite the opposite. Neither Helen nor I had thin frames, and while this wasn't a secret to anyone (including ourselves), our classmates quickly defaulted to addressing us as hippos and elephants as a way to reinforce the idea that we took up too much space. Our first names were publicly and permanently substituted with the names of voluminous creatures because of the size of our bodies—an intentionally cruel indication that we were nothing more than monstrous creatures. We were surreptitiously deemed grotesque miscreants by our classmates *simply because of our weight.*

The relationship I've had with my body over the years is complicated and full of nuanced details that would take hundreds of pages to thoroughly explain, but if I were to summarize the most prominent theme that has dictated how I feel about my physical self, it would be this: I hated my body since the moment I was capable of understanding what the word *fat* meant in our society. The realization that *fat* was one of the worst things that you could be happened long before I found myself with a designated nickname in fifth grade. Simply put: I have spent the vast majority of my life living in a mental state of extraordinary self-loathing, and it has impacted how I've participated in the world in almost every way.

It was also around middle school that I began my decade-long habit of chronic dieting, dedicating my entire life to shrinking my body— everything else that I did became secondary in importance. Every waking moment revolved around trying to lose weight, even before my body had a chance to fully develop. I tried it all, from starvation to SlimFast to dangerous phentermine pills that were eventually pulled from the market for causing heart valve damage. I would binge and then promptly throw it all up in the bathroom. I lived off rice cakes for weeks at a time and even tried a program that guaranteed weight loss through replacing your need for food with a love for Jesus. This dangerous and disordered eating continued well into my twenties, as I attempted one "surefire" diet after another. I physically and mentally harmed my body over and over, never trusting its need for nutrition or my brain's need for balance and self-compassion.

Convinced that obsessive dieting wasn't enough (in addition to the fact that dieting doesn't and didn't work), I tried to compensate for my perceived failure by being the best in every other area of my life. I did whatever it took to ensure I had the highest grades, tried to be the best at every sport my parents enrolled me in (there were dozens), and overextended myself in every area of life to the point of having nervous breakdowns . . . simply because I felt "just being myself" wasn't good enough. I was certain that I was deeply flawed because my body never looked like the "ideal bodies" that I idolized in every magazine I read. I spent my life constantly feeling sorry for my close friends, often pitying them for being forced to endure the company of my body just so they could hang out with the rest of me. I internalized every lie that told me I was undeserving of happiness and dated people who reinforced my negative self-views, eventually finding a long-term partner who left me because I had gained weight over the years we had been together. It was only after this final, soul-crushing relationship that I found a way to halt my self-harm: I experienced the radical revelation that there might be another way to live.

This life-altering revelation came in the surprising form of a simple blog.

In my midtwenties I found *The Nearsighted Owl*, a lifestyle website written by Rachele, a woman who rocked fabulous cat-eye glasses. I instantly identified with her love of vintage thrifting, owls, delicious recipes, cats, and purple beehives—but there was one glaring difference between her and me. Rachele and I were both fat—that was something we did have in common. But *unlike* me, Rachele was fat, confident, and *happy*. This unequivocal distinction left me speechless.

This was the first time in my life that I had ever witnessed a woman who lived in a fat body *and also* lived a life chock-full of joy, love, and empowerment. It was her unapologetic writing and lifestyle that spurred the revolutionary thought that changed my life's direction forever: *Maybe I don't have to hate myself for the rest of my life.*

Maybe I don't have to hate myself for the rest of my life! Maybe I can even sort of . . . like myself!?! Rachele was doing it, so perhaps I could, too.

Rachele was my introduction into the world of "Fat Acceptance," a universe that had existed my entire life and was based around the concept that ALL bodies—no matter their shape, size, weight, age, ability, race, ethnicity, or health status—deserved rights, respect, and unadulterated freedom. Finding Rachele's blog—finding fat acceptance—helped me see a better future. Maybe you've had that experience when looking at Snapchat or browsing Instagram: someone with a body like yours publicly and unabashedly living their best life. Just the simple act of witnessing their confidence has the potential to change everything. It certainly did for me.

Because of Rachele, I finally grasped a new, undeniable truth: Fat bodies were just as worthy as every other body. The truth was, I could have a life full of love and joy without needing to hate or shrink my body. The truth was, fat was neither a bad thing nor a bad word—and *this truth was intoxicating.*

I dove headfirst into this newfound reality, one that became even more compelling as I explored further. I followed radical Tumblr accounts, purposefully sought out photos of diverse bodies, and I read every fat acceptance book I could find. I researched the history of body image, studied the real facts around fat and health (spoiler: Everything the world thinks it knows about fatness and health is wrong), and joined a community of other people who were as invested in body acceptance as I was. I eventually started to notice something wonderful—the more I learned about body acceptance, the more my perception of the world shifted. I found myself becoming less judgmental—not just of others, but also of my own body. I was reformatting my reality. I was rewiring my belief in acceptability. I was finally teaching myself the truth.

And it was through all this that I harnessed the limitless power that can come by reclaiming the word *fat.*

This word, while something that I'm happy to use, still makes many others deeply uncomfortable. Their discomfort often causes them to jump to my "defense" by saying things like, "No way, Jes! You're just chubby. Fluffy. Curvy. Plus-size. You're *insert every other socially preferred euphemism here.*" To those friends I say: I know you think I'm insulting myself when I say that I'm fat, but here's why I prefer to use the "f word" more than any other descriptor: The word *fat* is not inherently bad. It's a simple adjective. It's a neutral descriptor of the size of my body. And while others may choose to use other words to describe their large bodies (and it is certainly their right to do so), the act of personally reclaiming *fat* resonated with me on a cellular level.

Yes, I am compassionate, tattooed, creative, loyal, determined, short, musical, strong, energetic, and a million other things. I'm also decidedly fat.

Saying "I'm fat" is (and should be) the same as saying the ocean is wet, my favorite dress is green, dirt is gritty, and Emma Watson's hair is brown. It's not a good thing, it's not a bad thing, it simply is what it is.

Here is the simple reality that took me years to learn: The only negativity that the word *fat* carries is the negativity that we have created around it. Our disgust when it comes to fat bodies is 1,000 percent learned. This may sound surprising, but we don't actually need to stop using the word *fat* because we think it's a negative depiction. We need to stop the hatred that we connect with the word instead.

It's the dots we connect between the word and someone's worth that is harmful, and THAT is the part we must change.

I now use it often because I have decided that it's officially MY word to wield, and the more I use it positively, the more fat stigma I smash. I've found that calling myself fat has become an empowering way to walk through this world. When someone tries to insult me by calling me fat, I just say, "I sure am! And?"

After my introduction to the body positivity and fat acceptance movements (there are multiple facets to the body image world, and these are two of the prominent ones), I started my own body image blog: *The Militant Baker*, where I chronicled my own journey and dedicated myself to always being authentic and sharing the vulnerable parts of life that we often feel scared to offer the world. *The Militant Baker* has since been described as "raw, honest, and attitude-filled." I'm flattered by this in every way.

I've since launched two internationally attended body image conferences, given nearly one hundred lectures at universities and events across the world, written two books, held healing body image photo shoots for more than two hundred people, appeared in multiple documentaries and television shows, worked with dozens of plus-size clothing companies, have been covered by more than three hundred national and international media outlets, written more than five hundred body image and mental health related articles, and posted (approximately) seventy public pictures of me in my underwear as well as a few that showcase my fat body in the nude.

I am fully aware of how privileged I am to be able to participate in this kind of work; my success is in large part because I am a cisgender, white, able-bodied woman, and the world accepts most of me with a few scant exceptions. It's this privilege that has allowed me to have a large platform with multiple outlets. And it's that platform that affords me the opportunity to preach about the importance of body liberation, self-advocacy, mental health, and diversity and intersectionality, as well as other hard conversations, strong coffee, and even stronger language.

I'm lucky as hell, and I know it.

Fifth grade may have been the first time I was called an animal name as an attempted insult, but it certainly wasn't the last. As a hypervisible fat person on the Internet, I'm still called all sorts of animal names online by strangers who know nothing about me except for the fact that they vehemently dislike the body I live in. What amazes me most is that these insults haven't improved or become more creative since I was ten years old and wore socks the color of which was nothing short of fashionably offensive to every other fifth grader.

Grown adults (sometimes twice my age) still take the time to find their way into my social media comment sections—and occasionally my inbox, if they're extra ambitious!—so that they can leave a delightful comment about how much I resemble a whatever-animal-they-think-is-the-most-insulting-to-be-compared-to before they move on to harass the next person they've dedicated their life to tormenting online. Obviously, these individuals haven't matured much beyond my dear friend Danielle, but they don't seem to notice the embarrassment that should accompany these kinds of mundane and childish comments.

There are certainly comments that do hurt me, comments that penetrate the emotional boundaries that I have consciously and internally built, reminding me that I am more than my body . . . but animal names? Especially animal names that are easily reframed as compliments given that the animals in question are, quite frankly, incredible creatures? Those no longer harm me, in the same way that calling me fat no longer wounds me.

It was this reframing of animal-based insults that inspired the title of my second book: *Landwhale*. (Other versions of this include: Orca, Shamu, Free Willy, Beluga, or sometimes just a whale emoji if the commenter is feeling particularly careless.)

Once, *whale* was a dreaded nickname to a chubby teen who wore giant T-shirts over her swimsuit when we visited the ocean. I've since learned how amazing whales are and what an honor it is to be compared to one. Some cool whale facts: They can talk to each other through song and effortlessly leap out of the ocean. The blue whale is the largest animal to EVER exist. And they all basically run the ocean, which covers 71 percent of the earth. Not to mention, a narwhal (which is totally a whale but never seems to make the insult list) is literally an underwater *unicorn*.

Can you see how calling me a whale is ACTUALLY one of the greatest compliments? And this goes for just about every other animal name I've been called.

I've learned over the years that when these kinds of insults are hurled my way, it is a simple but desperate attempt to dehumanize me and my existence. I'm often additionally called an "it" online so that people can pile on the verbal abuse without the inconvenience of acknowledging that I'm a sentient and complex human being. It took a while to realize that these sorts of labels have nothing to do with my worth as a person, but rather everything to do with the other person's lack of self-esteem and their internalized fatphobia, neither of which are my responsibility to take on. *A happy person doesn't try to ruin another person's happiness.* This is a fundamental truth that I keep in mind when someone hurts me; I hope that you can eventually do the same.

Fortunately, we now live in a time when millions of people are waking up to the reality that dieting, exclusive beauty standards, and body hatred is a megascam all created by industries dedicated to breaking us down, stealing our self-esteem, and then turning their theft around to sell us products to "fix" the problem that they purposefully created.

Can you see how calling me a whale is ACTUALLY one of the greatest compliments? And this goes for just about every other animal name I've been called.

I hope you can hear me when I tell you this truism: Our bodies are the size they are, and each and every size is more than OK. I mean this genuinely. Take it from a fat girl who has spent most of her life hating her body, dieting, and depriving herself of any sort of happiness because she believed those who told her she didn't deserve it, and now knows better.

This is not to say that every day is easy or that I don't fall back into old patterns of self-loathing. I have "bad body days" more often than I would like. I'm purposefully sharing these hard days with the Internet as well; the last thing I want is for those who are attempting to make peace with their body feel like failures because they haven't been able to achieve the ability to feel 100 percent positive when it comes to their own self-image.

We are all human, my friend. And we've spent most of our life learning lies. Those ideas aren't going to disappear overnight. I've come to realize that I will likely be relearning the lessons I share with others and working toward trusting my body and its inherent value for the rest of my life. Relearning how to accept yourself is indeed a complicated recovery process, and recovery journeys are anything but linear. Recovery is also not a race, nor a destination you find quickly and never leave. The biggest difference between my past and present is the fact that I now know that I am an incredible human who deserves to live my best life, and I'm willing to put in the work it takes to get there.

It's critical we remember that words are far more powerful than most of us realize. Regardless of our age, the words we use (or don't use, out of fear) shape the way we think, act, and participate in the world. Knowing this in addition to learning over the years that ALL bodies are good bodies has shown me how meaningful the act of reclaiming words can be. The act of reclaiming words that have historically been associated with a negative connotation as positive or neutral descriptors (even using them cheekily is effective AF) strips them of the previous jurisdiction they held over our lives. This, consequently, also makes it impossible for others to use these words as weapons against us, which is a helluva impressive thing.

It's time for us to take our power back. For you to take your power back. You deserve to live a life that is free from shame and filled with freedom. Believe me when I say that you can start your own internal revolution by reclaiming and reframing one word at a time.

I hope the next time someone tries to insult you with that almighty f word, you're able to turn around, look them straight in the eye, and genuinely smile as you say, "And?"

JES BAKER

is a positive, progressive, and magnificently irreverent force to be reckoned with and is internationally known for preaching the importance of body liberation, self-love, mental health, strong coffee, and even stronger language as an author and blogger. When not writing, Jes spends her time speaking around the world, working as a body image and mental health coach, collaborating with plus-size clothing companies, organizing body liberation events, taking pictures in her underwear, and attempting to convince her cats that they like to wear bow ties. You can learn more about Jes through TheMilitantBaker.com and JesBaker.com.

Growing up, I filled my
life with comic books,
music, art, and movies
that made me feel good
about my body shape.

I'm grateful that those
creators embraced a
beauty that wasn't popular.
It shaped my self-confidence.

Love You
(an illustration)

by
MEL STRINGER

I was born in the 1980s and grew up in the 1990s. The ideal body shape was thin. Thin, skinny, tall and thin, gaunt facial features—everything I wasn't. Everything I didn't have. This ideal body type was reinforced through music clips, films, fashion (and clothes that would fit on this body type), and magazines (for both adults and teens). The list goes on.

Everywhere I looked, this body type was the epitome of beauty. But something inside me knew better. I knew that I was beautiful and attractive in my own way, and I carried myself confidently, even though I knew it wasn't a popular opinion for chubby girls to be beautiful (or to love themselves).

I slowly started to find curvy bodies like mine being portrayed in old paintings by Gauguin. I found artists like Sophie Campbell, Yoshitomo Nara, and Chris Sanders (creator of *Lilo & Stitch*). Beth Ditto and Kelly Osbourne inspired me, too, being the only big girls I'd ever seen in the music industry during my lifetime. These things helped reinforce my confidence. Now fast-forward to 2018, and you can see all sorts of curvy bodies everywhere, and I feel great that young women have so many places to turn to see a body like theirs. I hope my art adds to the confidence of curvy women. One body type is no longer the epitome of beauty. It's different now, and I love that.

MEL STRINGER

is an Australian-born visual artist and comic creator currently based in Missouri. She expresses herself through her very body-positive art focused on fashionable babes, while her diary comics are her go-to for documenting her real life.

To All the Pizzas I've Loved Before

by
LAINA SPENCER

I've been more sexually attracted to pizza than to people. What does that even mean? I am aromantic and asexual, or aroace. If you have never heard those labels before, that means I don't feel sexual or romantic attraction. Others on the aro and ace spectrums (a-spec) might feel attraction rarely, or only under certain circumstances, but I don't.

Pictures of a supercheesy pepperoni pizza have been sexier to me than pictures of a superhot person. That's a joke, see, because I'm fat. And it's funny, because I'm making it. It's not funny when it comes in the form of, "You're fat, so no one would want you anyway." I don't want a sexual or romantic relationship. I'm fat. Neither of those mean you get to insult me. And frankly if it were true that being fat made me undesirable, I'd have to deal with a lot fewer creeps.

Being fat can be a lonely club sometimes. Sometimes you feel like you're the only one, even though it's a club with billions of members. Being fat and a-spec is an even smaller club. When you seek out safe spaces, you can find yourself being treated as an afterthought. If you're spending time in a fat-activism space, it can sometimes be very romance- and sex-focused, which aren't things that make me feel included. A-spec-focused spaces aren't automatically friendly to fat people. And the thing is, it is impossible to divide yourself into acceptable little pieces, no matter what the parts that you're made up of are. You can never cut yourself small enough to please everyone. You aren't a cheese platter. People can't pick and choose the parts they like best and ignore the rest of you. If one part of you is hurt, all of you hurts.

It hurts to not see yourself represented, or to always see yourself represented negatively. Anyone of a marginalized identity understands this. I love to read, and, like anyone, I've looked for characters like me in the books I read. Books with fat characters are thankfully becoming more common, especially in YA, where fat-positive novels are on the rise. Books with a-spec characters are much less common in mainstream publishing, especially in YA, though indie books are thriving. Traditional publishing is slower to get there. And when you combine those things? Seeing myself represented as both fat and a-spec happens incredibly rarely.

You might find it interesting that I write books with romance in them and enjoy reading them as well. Sex, too. (While many ace and aro people want and have sex or romance, those are not things I am personally interested in.) One of my absolute favorite books is *The Summer of Jordi Perez* by Amy Spalding, which has a wonderful relationship between two girls, one of whom is fat. Reading books where fat characters have romance and are attractive to other characters makes me happy a lot of the time.

In fact, when I was a teenager, I identified more as demiromantic, feeling romantic attraction only once a bond has been formed. I had a few crushes growing up, but they were very few and far between. As I got older that pretty much stopped happening. And looking back, even before I knew that label, I never really pictured romantic relationships actually happening with *me* as a participant. I thought that was normal, because I was fat, especially while I was still in high school. Of course I didn't want to date people who had bullied me for being fat. Who would want to date people who had been cruel to them like that? It was logical to me. What other explanations could there be? I thought things would change when I made it out into the "real" world and met people who were more accepting of my body.

Well, in a way, they did, but not exactly how I expected. When I got into fandom, I started spending more time on Tumblr, and I started hearing words for sexualities and genders that I had never heard before. Of course, I didn't think any of them applied to me.

Then I learned about the labels *asexual* and *aromantic*. Suddenly there were words for what I was! It wasn't just something I was doing wrong, or because there was something wrong with me. There were words for me, and it was OK. And around the same time, I was becoming more involved in fat activism, where I was being told the word *fat* wasn't actually a bad word, or even a bad thing to be. I didn't need to dance around a description of my body or only use so-called flattering descriptions like *curvy* or *plump* to talk about myself. I'm aromantic. I'm asexual. I'm fat. I'm also short, allergic to dust, and a bit of a book hoarder. These are some of the parts of me that make the whole. Even if people don't like them, I do, and I'm the only one who gets a vote.

While I still enjoy books where fat people have romance, I don't want that to be the only option. I wish when I was a teenager there had been more books about fat people living their best lives, whether that included romance or prioritizing a life full of meaningful relationships with family and friends. Or even books that featured fat characters getting up to exciting adventures that had nothing to do with their interpersonal relationships.

If you are fat and you want a romantic or sexual relationship, that is absolutely a thing you are allowed to have, and don't ever accept anything less than a partner who treats you with respect and care. And you will be able to find someone. But it's also important to know that you don't *have* to want that. Your body is not a good body because someone else is attracted to it. Your body is a good body because it's a beautiful, amazing fat body. You can live a full, wonderful life whether you want romantic or sexual relationships or not. Being fat and a-spec might be a small club, but we're awesome.

And I promise, the pizza here is amazing.

LAINA SPENCER

is an aspiring YA author who writes a lot of books about queerness, fatness, and murder. Only two of those she has personal experience with, she promises. She has an ongoing project to analyze L. M. Montgomery's library of work and co-runs Queer Summer Reading, an online book club that aims to promote reading queer literature. You can find her on Twitter as @lainasparetime and online at lainaspencer.wordpress.com.

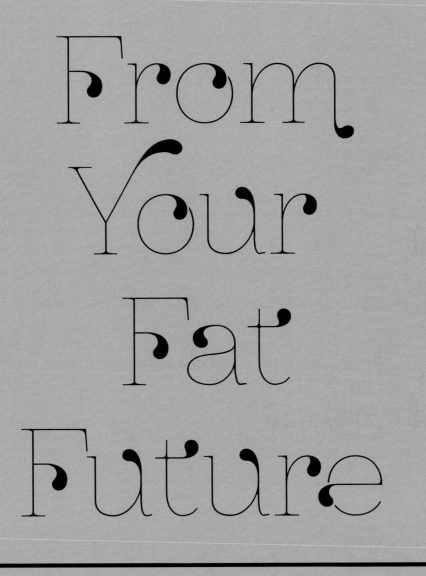

From Your Fat Future

by
ADRIANNE RUSSELL

Dear Adrianne (and sorry you still can't find stuff with your name at gift shops),

You're seventeen and you know a lot about a lot of things—more that you don't—even though you'd never admit it to anyone. You look like your shit is completely together and your desire to not stick out too much from the crowd is super strong, almost as strong as your need to be noticed.

You're part of a well-to-do family and have a nice house, a cute football-playing boyfriend, excellent grades, and your own car. You have all the things a person would expect to need in order to be happy—except you're fat.

And I get it, it's not like you hate yourself every second of the day, but you're surrounded by so many things that make you feel different. At your school, you're one of less-than-a-handful of Black students (people assume you're in your all-girls prep school on hardship or due to the benevolence of good white folk), and everyone else is so petite and white and privileged and seemingly has every possible advantage just laid at their feet. You're angrier about it than anyone knows. You're frustrated. And you figure that there's so much that you can't change—your skin, racism, your family pedigree—but you can do something about the way your body looks.

Because in your eyes, your body is a betrayal. You think it's the way it is because of something you've done. Been too smart-mouthed, too lazy, too needful, too greedy, too prideful. Otherwise it means that it's simply an inexplicable combination of genetics or fate or just who-knows-what and this is just how you were meant to be and that is unacceptable. Every cause has an effect. And if something you've done made you this way, it can be undone.

(And I know it feels like everything is this black-and-white and will be forever, but I promise you, life will be lived mostly in that messy gray middle.)

So, despite three-hour daily varsity volleyball practices, you decide to add two more hours of working out at home. You try prepackaged food plans and those nasty shake meal replacements. Sometimes it even works, at least for a little while. You manage to subdue your body's betrayal. But it never lasts, and you get super frustrated when you end those programs and whatever pounds you dropped creep back on. You're tired mentally and physically and you're so dang hungry all the time, you can barely think straight.

You feel like your body is the enemy, something apart from you, that doesn't belong to you. Every moment is a struggle, a fight to reconcile who you think you are with who you think you want to be. Your mind, housed in this body you despise, suffers so much. You're upset that as smart as you are, you can't figure out how to solve this problem. That as determined as you are, you keep failing. It's frustrating and infuriating, especially because you're used to winning, to achieving goals. The formula seems so simple: eat less, move more. But it just isn't working.

You're determined to control the uncontrollable, but it's a losing game. And not in the way you think you want, in pounds and inches, but in the small bits of your spirit and sense of self that diminish with every effort. There are so many reasons you are trying to control your weight and bring your body into submission. You're doing it because you think it will make your boyfriend treat you better. You're doing it because you think you're ruining your family's image. You're doing it because everything in our society tells you it's the key to happiness.

And sis, guess what? You're wrong. But that's OK, too. You'll find out being wrong isn't the end of the world. And you're gonna get so many opportunities to make it right.

Your determination in pursuit of this goal is detrimental, to be sure. But what you need to know is this trait, when channeled toward productive, positive pursuits, is one of your greatest superpowers. Your ability to adapt, to problem-solve, to find joy in both simplicity and grandeur, is going to carry you so, so far.

I know this because I am writing to you from your fat future. I want to tell you a little about what it's like here. Please know that your body is still sometimes a mystery. It's thrown you a few curveballs (while also developing awesome new curves) and you've made it through. Once you realize that associating happiness with your appearance is bunk, the world opens. Being fat is no longer a curse or a punishment. Your body isn't the enemy. It's your partner, your home,

your vessel in which you go through life. Even when it does something you can't control, you don't want to hurt it or shape it into something else. You work with it to find a solution, to treat it as well as you can, to ensure its survival. You nurture talents, develop skills, have adventures. You meet people you can't imagine moving through this world without, but you know that if that time came—if things with those people didn't work out—that's not your body's fault. Our fat future is marvelous because despite all the things we've gone through, we survived, thrived, and never stopped dreaming.

You're going to encounter negativity in many forms, from people you know and trust and strangers alike, and it's gonna hurt like hell, but you're going to make it through.

And your body, the thing you think is holding you back, is gonna hold you up. It's gonna hold you down. It's a source of strength, of comfort, for yourself and for others. You'll learn to care for it out of love rather than fear. See it as a thing of wondrous beauty. And you'll be grateful, so grateful, that you inhabit it.

ADRIANNE RUSSELL

has spent most of her life making things up, and the only thing she loves more than reading grand adventures is writing them. She fully believes that if you're unsure what to do with your characters, having them kiss or fight (and occasionally both) will unstick any plot. When she's not managing library book groups, she's usually napping, watching movies, and advocating for marginalized voices in children's literature. You can find her writing at auto8collective.com.

Fat. Boy. Walking.

by
MIGUEL M. MORALES

My arms slide through sleeves as my large head pops through the stretched neckhole. Socks slip onto my wide feet. Thick fingers tie worn shoelaces followed by the simple string inside the elastic waistband of my shorts. Earbuds secured. Fitness app launched. I select my playlist: Werk Out.

I'm not going to lie, I don't do this every day. Walking to the park a few blocks away, my body feels strange. It's in motion, uncoordinated, lunging, and pounding the sidewalk. I want to turn around and go back home, where I'm safe and unseen. I'm certain that I look as stupid as I feel.

Slowly my feet slide into the music's rhythm. My legs and thighs soon follow. My husky hips rock side to side as my belly smoothly sways, giving me momentum. My arms swing at my sides, keeping stride. My body's rhythm moves up into my chest.

My fat bounces and shimmies to the rhythmic clave it has created. Each song from my playlist brings on a fresh sassy strut. With each new step, my body follows my commands, sensing and trusting the rhythm we've established, the dance we're creating. I've always loved dancing. Why did I stop?

As I walk uphill, my center of gravity shifts to my lower back, causing my bountiful bottom to extend farther out, slowing my rhythm. My hamstrings and nalguitas propel and elevate me. Pumping arms help quicken my breathing. I exhale a steady beat.

Standing atop the summit, my body finds its previous balance. The breeze ignites a cool fire on my sweaty neck and down my back that quickly extinguishes itself. I survey my surroundings, taking in nature's celebrated largeness, its fatness, feeling confident in my own.

Walking downhill, my lower spine tilts forward again, shifting my center of gravity. I smile at every bounce and jiggle of my fat. Hefty legs steady my momentum. My body undulates to this new harsh, indigenous rhythm. Moving now toward home, my body anticipates each step.

My torso slightly twists, keeping time with my body's own bachata. Invigorated strangers on the park's path nod hello to me. They smile, offering thumbs-up encouragement. I nod in return, knowing, my dear fats, I'm no longer walking to shed weight, to become smaller. It may have started that way.

Instead, I'm walking to experience my body in a different way than I do when I'm at work or driving or with friends. I'm walking to enliven my muscles and my bones and my fat and feel them working, no, dancing . . . yes . . . so I can feel all of them as we dance—together.

Reasons to Hang in There

by
SAMANTHA IRBY

1

Seeing Your Enemies Fail

I'm petty. I know I'm not supposed to admit it or whatever, but literally WHAT is the point of staying alive and trying to succeed if not to receive a friend request from some asshole who made fun of your gym shorts? Then to scroll through his pictures and look at his gross dog and his weird kids and remember how hard he made your life twenty years ago. And meanwhile his current life, the life he actually put together himself rather than the one that was forced upon him by his broke and unprepared parents, is garbage?! It is the most satisfying feeling, and I'm not sorry for having it! Whatever I looked like or did/didn't have in the seventh grade was definitely not my fault. I didn't have a job! I couldn't make the rules! Would I have *chosen* to buy bright pink Payless sneakers while everyone else was rocking brand-new Jordans? No, sir, I would not have. But I was twelve. He paid for that shitty haircut *and* he posted a picture of it on his Twitter? Thanks for this much-needed validation! So, trust me, it's going to happen for you, too. And it will feel like a unicorn sliding down a rainbow into your heart. Anyone who has wronged you will eventually get their comeuppance. And, thanks to modern technology, you'll probably get to watch it in real time.

2

Stocking Your Pantry Like an Adult Child

I'm not going to bullshit you and say that I never buy vegetables because listen, sometimes I read articles about how much folic acid a functioning body needs, and information about B vitamins worms its way into my tiny brain, and I think, "Wow, I should buy spinach" while strolling through the cereal aisle at the grocery store; but honestly the Oreo-to-carrot ratio in my house is a smooth 2:1. Sure, I buy hummus and the good kind of organic peanut butter. But I don't have any kids, and maybe having someone's behavior to monitor is the catalyst through which you begin to monitor your own, so I just get what I want, and no one's disapproving eyebrows will rise in judgment as I have cake for breakfast.

3

3 a.m. Is a Lie

When I was a kid, all I ever wanted to know was what happened in the adult universe after 9 p.m. As a rapidly decaying, expired bag of meat I have learned that it is not as scintillating as I once assumed. The universe is set up to trick you into believing that you aren't cool and that a magical trapdoor of awesome adventures swings open on your eighteenth birthday, or that everything that happens after you've already gone to bed is an unimaginable thrill ride, but let me disabuse you of these notions: Every titillating adult mystery is really just a hassle or a bill in disguise. No need to wish on your birthday candles for your exciting adult life to start, because you're perfect and so is your life as it is right this minute. Besides, adulthood is really nothing but drudgery and hard work masquerading as glamorous excitement, and nothing fun happens for the rest of us while you are young and dewy and going to bed before midnight. I promise you.

4

Talking Back to the Doctor

I mean, they're gonna say whatever the hell they're gonna say. And the power dynamic is skewed, especially if you're sitting there in that crumpled paper gown with the majority of your soft parts exposed. But instead of your legal guardian nodding solemnly along with whatever shitty thing they're saying about you while placing a silencing hand on your meaty backside, you can interrupt and remind them that you are a person, not just a collection of fat cells, and they need to address your concerns rather than condescendingly schooling you on how calories are burned. There's a growing understanding that being fat doesn't mean unhealthy, and there are HAES (health at every size) doctors who will listen to you and respect your body as it is, not as some outdated health manual dictates it should be. Seek out these doctors—the ones you feel comfortable with, who will respect what you're saying—especially because *you* know yourself best and should never be bullied into someone else's idea of how a person should be. Besides, anyone who has so much as glanced at women's magazines is basically an expert at weight loss, doc, now what about that ear infection I came in for?

Decorating Your Own Crib

Did you know that there are mattresses specifically for fat bodies? There are mattresses specifically for fat bodies!!! And you can buy one on your phone and have it delivered to your doorstep in a matter of days. Also, no more couches that your mom won't let you sit on. You can eat every meal in front of the TV if you want or mix up all your clothes in whatever cycle you want in the washing machine and balance all eight bottles of body wash on the edge of the tub because, *Hey, Mom, I LIKE A LITTLE VARIETY.* Don't put a coaster down! Or buy a table that's made of fucking coasters because who cares? It's your house! You no longer have to look at your brother's graduation photo every time you grab a Coke from the fridge. Hate having a dust ruffle? You don't have to have a goddamn dust ruffle!!

Empowering Shit on TV

I loved TV as a kid. Like, really loved it. And I had bad parents, so I was allowed to consume as much of it as I wanted, unsupervised, most hours of the day. But we didn't have cable, and "streaming services" were a far-off invention of the future ("the inter-WHAT?!"—my mom, probably), so most of the shit I watched was relatively wholesome: cartoons in the morning, *All My Children* in the afternoons, whatever was on the NBC prime-time lineup at night. Nowadays everybody's worried about screen time, and I get it, there's physics homework to do. But we're also just at the beginning of this golden age of television, where fat people are making shows about being fat and unapologetic, and it's just going to get better.

Imagine what kind of bad bitch I could be if teenage me had had *Dietland* in my life?! I mean, *Heathers* did a pretty good job of raising me, but *The Mindy Project* might have gotten me into a better college. Just saying.

7

Seeing the Character-Building Experiences of Your Youth in Action

Every day at the beginning of gym class this kid used to ask me, in a way that on the surface seemed like genuine curiosity but I knew he was actually being a dick, "Hey, how much do you weigh?" Truth be told, I had no fucking idea because my parents never took me to the fucking doctor and we weren't a "this scale actually works" kind of household; so when I told him that I didn't know, that was the honest truth. But I knew what he was getting at: that whatever my weight was, it was DEFINITELY TOO MUCH. At the time that shit just bummed me out and made me throw two-thirds of my lunch into the trash in the vain hope that not consuming six nuggets and a lukewarm milk every Tuesday would result in some lasting weight loss. But now I think that asshole is the reason why I can wear a crop top to the gas station without batting a single eyelash when people gawk or give me those, "Hey, good for you!" looks. It didn't feel like it then, but that dude was just helping me build my armor, one plate at a time.

8

Plus-Size Clothing Is Marginally Better Now!!!

I'm almost mad at every single person reading this right now who never had to wear an ankle-length, acid-washed denim skirt from Sears to middle school, but I'm gonna stifle that hatred and find the part of me that is genuinely happy that you can be a size twenty-six and find things to wear that don't make you look like you live on a compound. Especially if you don't have an unlimited clothing budget. And I know that looking like warmed-up shit is a rite of passage, and if you've embraced it—WOW I LOVE THAT—but also, hey, look at that cute crop top!

9

Sexing (and Other Consensual Corporeal Touching)

I don't know that I grew up with the kinds of TV villains we've grown accustomed to (popped pastel collars, windblown hair sprayed to within an inch of its life, 1987 convertibles), but I *did* grow up thinking that no one was ever gonna want to see my body naked, and that even if they did, it surely would have been as part of some hilarious prank and not because an actual human being wanted to bring it to orgasm. I didn't ever date anyone when I was a kid, and maybe it's because I have a shitty personality. But at the time it definitely felt like it was because I was FAT. And not just fat, but fat and wearing men's slacks with buffalo-checked flannel shirts. No one wanted to kiss me! But then I graduated and moved the fuck on and then I couldn't stop being kissed, by all kinds of people! And not because I had some magical Cinderella makeover or hatched from my disgusting cocoon a beautiful butterfly. No, I was fatter and weirder than ever before, and that was appealing to people outside of my high school. I had no idea that there was an entire world of people who just couldn't wait to wrap their arms around my many doughy folds. And if that's not your thing? That's fine, too! There are so many people who will respect that and like you and want to chill with you no matter what you and your boundaries look like.

10

Your Body Is Just Fine. You Know That, Right?

If there's one thing I wish someone would have said to teenage me as I shuffled over the shiny linoleum floors of my suburban high school in steel-toe Doc Martens and an ever-present sulk, it would be, "Listen,

dude, your body is fine." We were poor, so I used to buy my clothes at the Salvation Army, and it's not like I could have been in charge of my own style anyway. But it was fucking *impossible* when I was limited to whatever five-dollar big 'n' tall dress pants and collared shirts I could scrounge up in the husky section. And it's hard to feel confident and good in your body when everything is changing and hormones are raging just below the surface of your skin. But add to that general awkwardness a lumpy, hairy, acne-prone body that isn't reflected kindly on TV or the Internet or in magazines and LOL WHAT IS SELF-ESTEEM AGAIN?! But it really is OK; and I need you to really know this, for you to enjoy the body you have right now. To just be cool moving it around and allowing it to be whatever it is, without apologizing for whatever space it takes up. I have no real idea of exactly how to do this, because I'm thirty-nine years old and still find myself apologizing for my horrifyingly damp and awkward existence. But a thing I say in my head on an embarrassingly regular basis is, "This is the body you have, man. Go live your life." There was definitely a time when I thought that I couldn't start living until I magically woke up in my body a third of its normal size—that good things wouldn't happen for me until, I don't know, my fat wrists got smaller?! Yet here I am, cheeks as chubby as they've ever been, and I'm fine. I do fun shit that makes me happy every single day. My friends love me. My body continues to serve its many purposes, chief among them carting this brain and heart around.

So never forget that you're good. You really are! Keep your (many) chins up.

EVA BLUE

SAMANTHA IRBY

writes a blog called *bitches gotta eat.*

Baltimore . . . and Me

by
AMY SPALDING

The thing about being fat is that—at least for me and the fat people in my life—it never seemed to match what I heard about fat people. Fat people I knew were smart, interesting, passionate, and a thousand other qualities that couldn't be traced back to any fat joke I'd ever been told. They were athletic . . . or not. Happily relationshipped . . . or not. Highly educated . . . or not. In other words, they represented a vast and diverse human experience, just like everyone else. So, if the stereotypes about laziness and stupidity didn't line up with my real-life experience, where was this even coming from?

I wish there was a simple pathway from the origin of fatphobia to its often-devastating results, so that fat people and allies could home in on it and easily burst it apart with knowledge and empathy. Look, I'm the author of books about cute teens having swoony experiences, not a social scientist, so I realize a discussion regarding fatphobia in modern culture and its various root causes and effects are beyond my capabilities. I'm so glad those conversations are happening; I'm constantly grateful for anyone embarking on fat studies, and for all the fat activists who've gotten people to see this is something worth taking seriously.

But I don't think it takes a social scientist to understand where misunderstanding, stereotypes, and even downright hate are coming from. Just the experience of living as a fat person teaches you quite a bit about why the world sees us the way that it does. And something that's hard *not* to learn? As far as pop culture goes, we might as well not exist.

Of course, I've often thought that not existing in media sounded great in comparison to the representations of fat people I was used to. The one I think of the most is that crowd footage of headless fat people frequently used by local news stations to talk about stories ranging from so-called obesity epidemics to cholesterol medicine updates. There was never a camera angle that included any faces; these headless fats let you know the only thing worse than being fat was having the public know you were fat. Who were we supposed to think these fat bodies were attached to? Where were the headless fats going? What did the release form say when a cameraman pointed the lens at them? I guess none of this mattered to anyone, because if you don't think of fat people as fully three-dimensional humans, what does it matter? Three-dimensional people typically have heads, after all, and clearly these fats didn't. It sure is easy to reduce people to stereotypes when you dehumanize them entirely.

For the record, all the fat people I'm lucky enough to know have heads.

Yeah, yeah, that's just B-roll footage on nightly news stories; and who even watches the local news these days, am I right? But in scripted entertainment, I never felt like fat people fared any better. Maybe worse! At least the headless fats looked like they had somewhere to go and other fat people to walk, if not talk, with. Hopefully they had a support group. Hopefully that footage was captured on their way to the coolest party ever.

Fat characters on TV and in movies didn't get to go to cool parties, unless it was purely as a vehicle to spoil the fun for the main—always thin—characters. Fat characters never seemed to understand how much space they took up, frequently knocking over valuable, fragile items—or even other people. Never mind that I and every other single fat person I knew took incredible care to take up as little space as possible and stay away from restrictive areas. Fictional fat people were always showing up where they weren't wanted, like termites or one of those springy snakes that pops out of a can bearing the label MIXED NUTS, with no regard for the feelings of the poor, innocent thin people who might have to suffer a tragedy as great as having to interact with a fat person. Can you imagine?

I'd love to say that this didn't get to me, that the drastic difference between my real life as a fat person with friends I loved and a job I loved and a whole inner world that I—well, liked enough, was striking enough that I could just disregard fictional fats. But I'd be lying, because I hated every single part of this. I hated seeing bodies like mine used as fear-baiting. I hated being in a movie theater and realizing I was surrounded by people who laughed uproariously at the image of fat people being stupid, inconsiderate, and *somehow incapable of understanding basic human physics like what kind of chairs one's butt could feasibly fit into.*

For the record, I always know what kind of chairs my butt can fit into.

Even when a piece of pop culture happened to feature a fat person with a fully-developed inner life and a not-terrible outer life—progress!—their weight was, nearly without fail, presented as something they were unhappy with, something that they actively hated about themselves. The people who looked like me . . . hated that about themselves. And no matter what your own life looks like and how relatively healthy your self-esteem might be, it was a pretty terrible feeling.

It can wear you down to be consistently shown that loving yourself isn't an option. In the mirror and around my loved ones, I felt fine. Our culture isn't necessarily kind to women and their appearance in general, but most of the time that's about where I hovered—not much higher or lower than women of any given size. I'd have concerns about my hair or if this denim wash was too last season, but I didn't often step out of the house and worry about my size.

My size was a neutral thing on its own, until it wasn't. Because seeing a woman my same size as some sort of problem to be solved didn't keep my self-esteem at that hovering level. Was everyone thinking that about me? The friends, family, coworkers I'd felt comfortable and safe with—was that a lie? And if all these people I respected might secretly think I was only some "before," some problem to solve . . . was I? Deep down, I knew I had value, just as I was. But there were days when it was tough remembering that.

By the time the musical version of *Hairspray* was released as a film, I'd already seen the show on Broadway. I was fortunate enough to attend on a night less than one week out from the show's Tony wins, and so it felt both historic and inspiring to watch Marissa Jaret Winokur as the fat lead character, Tracy Turnblad. But the stage has always been its own thing to me. Since I was young, theater had space for characters of all colors in ways I wasn't necessarily seeing in mainstream film or television. The stage had roles for actresses over thirty, forty, fifty, and beyond. The stage gave us complex queer characters. And so, while I loved seeing Tracy fight not only for her own representation but in the much larger battle to desegregate early-1960s television, it didn't seem to bring us any closer to better representations of fat people in the media. After all, the musical was based on a movie from 1988. Things hadn't gotten magically better then. I hardly thought a Broadway musical seen by fewer people could get us there.

Then the *Hairspray* musical movie happened.

I'll begin with a blanket caveat that the movie is far from perfect. Stage to screen adaptations are always tricky, and I'm not the biggest fan of every cast member's performance. But, oh my god, how I love this movie anyway.

When Nikki Blonsky appears on-screen in the film's opening song, "Good Morning, Baltimore," I could hardly believe it. This wasn't an actress who weighed a few more pounds than the average female movie star. This was an actress whose body took up space in the same way mine did. But Tracy wasn't a punch line, and Tracy wasn't a joke. It was an exuberant paean from Tracy to her hometown of Baltimore, the city she loved and that clearly loved her right back. It was also a love letter to herself, her talents, and her own ambitions. This wasn't just a fat girl existing; this fat girl took joy in her skills. This fat girl was determined to get what she wanted.

Also, Tracy looked great. It wasn't what struck me most, though, about her appearance. Nope, that was how Blonsky embodied a girl who loved herself. There's a pride and a confidence Tracy takes in just those few moments of getting ready for school that told me everything I needed to know. Tracy was the film's heroine, and she wasn't supposed to hate herself like those ding-dongs in bad comedies whose self-love is seen more like self-delusion. Here was a girl built a whole lot like me, and she was the centerpiece of a movie that loved her and saw her story as valuable.

Tracy also wasn't, you know, just fat. In fact, just like me, most of her inner world re-

volved around completely unrelated things. Tracy loved to dance and was incredible at dancing. Tracy loved her friends, old and new, loudly and wholeheartedly. Tracy saw injustice in the world and realized that no matter what she got to achieve as a fat white girl, racism was an insidious hatred that had to be fought. And, sometimes most of all, Tracy daydreamed about ending up with Link Larkin, who wasn't a bore the fat girl had to settle for, but the cutest boy in all of Baltimore.

Once Tracy achieves her dream of dancing on the *Corny Collins Show,* Tracy and her mom, Edna, are given the opportunity to outfit themselves at Mr. Pinky's plus-size boutique, Hefty Hideaway. For basically my entire life, fashion magazines told me that the most "flattering" way for fat women to dress was

to "minimize" their size. Silhouettes should be draped, and colors should be dark, almost like you could blend into some black curtains and disappear. Yet the outfits Tracy and Edna receive from Hefty Hideaway are the opposite of subtle in silhouette and color. Zebra print! Glitter! Fringe! Sometimes all at once. If anything, size and curves are emphasized, because it turns out if you don't equate bigger measurements with moral failure, ugliness, or worse, there's no reason to pretend you're smaller.

I remember how I felt the first time I walked into a Torrid or the time period where ModCloth finally started carrying sizes above XL. I gave up wearing only some version of dark jeans with blouses that swooshed over me for candy-colored, twee-patterned A-line and fit-and-flare dresses that did absolutely nothing to make me look smaller. I wasn't small, and no number of drab patterns were going to change that. I might as well dress how I wanted, regardless. And *there's something about looking loud and in charge of your own look that can say a lot to the world,* because unfortunately it's still revolutionary to be fat and not hate yourself in public. When you wear something that won't "disappear" you into a dark curtain, even if it isn't covered in glitter or fringe, people get the message, subtle or otherwise, that you think you're someone worth seeing.

Tracy also—spoiler alert, for a twelve-year-old movie based on a thirty-one-year-old movie—gets the boy! She gets him as she is, and when he's weak-willed in the face of the powers that be, Tracy knows equality and her values matter way more than any cute boy with extremely good hair. But Baltimore's dreamy Link Larkin's no fool; he recognizes that Tracy and her beliefs are worth taking a stand for, and so it's a romance where the handsome-as-hell boy has to improve himself to deserve our heroine. Our fat heroine.

Look, I didn't only start wearing louder dresses because of Tracy and *Hairspray.* A lot of my love for Tracy was due to our existing similarities. I had always known I had a rich inner life—and no one who knows me would be surprised to hear I think Link Larkin's portrayer, Zac Efron, is super dreamy, especially back when he was singing and dancing all the goshdarn time. Friendship and family matter to me like they do to Tracy, and so does resistance. It wasn't that I needed her in order to know that about myself. I knew, inside, that I was more than any hacky joke, more than a fat body without a head. But Tracy gave me a mirror, and, in a way, I needed that to see myself fully. As I said, self-esteem can be hard for anyone. Getting a reminder that you can trust how you see yourself can be life-altering.

And there were real-life role models, too! Reading Lindy West and Roxane Gay gave me power in words, in vocabulary about fatness I didn't yet possess. Vocabulary can be a powerful weapon in the war against hating yourself. I still remember the first time that I referred to myself as fat to someone else and combatted their knee-jerk "Of course you're not fat!" with the simple fact that I was, and there wasn't anything wrong with that. In my day-to-day life I had in-person and text conversations with other fat women about our lives and our experiences. Connection is pretty powerful, too.

I still have a long way to go. When society still seems intent on letting fat people know how hated they are—if you don't believe me, look at the comments on any high-profile fat person's social media posts—I'm not immune. I take things to heart, and I feel crappy when a beautiful clothing item isn't made in my size. When people don't like me, even though I probably have dozens of actual bad qualities, I often assume it's because of my weight. Sometimes I hate photos of myself— maybe more than sometimes, if I'm being honest.

I'd be *lucky*, honestly, to be Tracy Turnblad. Not because she kisses Zac Efron or help ends racial segregation on television in Baltimore. It's because she believes that she deserves all the good things that happen to her. In fact, she fights for her spot on *Corny Collins* because she's well aware she's the best dancer. And it's not due to naivete on her part; Tracy knows the world sees her a certain way because she's fat, but it just doesn't hold her back because—if I may steal a phrase from the show itself—*you can't stop the beat.*

Pop culture didn't embrace Tracy so hard that they immediately gave fat girls the leads in all the hot new movies and network dramas. Probably one reason, in fact, I still think about Tracy as often as I do is that she still seems as rare, precious, and valuable as one of the objects fat characters break with their butts in hacky comedies. I dream of a world where entertainment is full of fat people: fat people who save the day, and fat people who screw things up for reasons completely unrelated to their fatness. Fat people falling in love, fat people unleashing evil schemes. Fats of all colors, genders, sexualities.

I'll always have Tracy, though, and the way I felt when I first saw her fatness on-screen. Maybe I'll never achieve the highs she reaches before she's even graduated high school, but representation in pop culture isn't only about hard truths or realism. Skinny people get to save the day and kiss the beautiful one *all the time* at the end of movies! They get to stand in for the very best versions of regular skinny people. They get to be cheered on by the world.

For the record, Tracy Turnblad made me feel that the very best version of myself was someone other people could cheer for, too.

ROBYN VON SWANK

AMY SPALDING

grew up in St. Louis but now lives in the better weather of Los Angeles. She has a BA in Advertising and Marketing Communications from Webster University and an MA in Media Studies from the New School. Amy studied long-form improv at the Upright Citizens Brigade Theatre. By day, she manages the digital media team for an indie film advertising agency. By later day and night, Amy writes, performs, and pets as many cats as she can. She is the author of five young adult novels, including her latest, the bestselling *The Summer of Jordi Perez (and the Best Burger in Los Angeles)*.

FAT FASHION resources

I gotta plug handmade **Size Queen Clothing**, from Bertha Pearl. The styles and colors are AMAZING, and she does custom work. Two words: hot pants!

Re/Dress is now only online but is still the home of teggings (between tights and leggings), which are amazingly stretchy and fit lots of bodies.

I know friends who love **Fat Fancy**, the vintage shop in Portland, Oregon.

I would love to give a shout-out to fat fleas for an amazing way to get cheap clothes and support community. Honestly, they're where most of my best clothing comes from. Fat fleas are location specific, which can be a bummer, but they're also amazing community events. And if you can get there, you can recoup travel costs for lots of amazing fashions in new and like-new condition. For example, you can get ten tops, five bottoms, and three dresses at Cupcakes and Muffintops for $96 (yeah, I know the prices). That's an entire work wardrobe for the price of a single dress in some places. Specifics change, but some long-standing ones are:

Oakland: **Cupcakes and Muffintops**

New York City: **The Big Fat Flea**

Boston: **The Big Thrifty**

I have friends in different places who get together for informal, cash-free clothing swaps. And if there isn't a swap happening near you, it just takes two or three people with similar fashion and size needs to get together and there you are, snagging new styles. Just bring what you're done with and take what you want. Donate the rest.

Yay fat clothes!

—Alex Gino

ASOS Men's Plus

DXL: Known for years for catering to an older audience, now they're offering a lot more modern and stylish clothing.

JCPenney Foundry Big & Tall: Also focused on a younger, modern audience.

Bonobos Extended Sizes

Also, check out the style and resources section of Chubstr.com. I've covered a TON of brands over the last nine years.

—Bruce Sturgell

Walmart: Fat clothing on a budget. My favorite.

Forever 21+: When there's spandex involved, it can fit up to a size 26.

Dia & Co: To learn what brands fit you and how is priceless!

Eloquii: For clothing that costs more but lasts longer. Work clothing especially!

—Jes Baker

In Australia, when I need something really nice, I go to **City Chic**. I like that they have clothes I can fit into, that make me feel comfortable and gorgeous. The alternative is going to **Target** and praying there'll be a size 20 on the rack. To be honest, **City Chic** can be a little pricey (for my tiny budget), but when I think about how often I wear each item of clothing, I know it's worth it.

—Jess Walton

I'm a **ASOS**/**Target**/**Old Navy** girl.

—Jonathan P. Higgins, Ed.D

CLOTHES I LOVE!

Rebdolls

City Chic

Asos Curve

CLOTHES I CAN AFFORD!

Avenue

Kohl's

Used clothing websites like **Poshmark**, **ThredUp**, **eBay**

CLOTHES I DREAM OF!

Igigi

Premme US

Jibri (Julie Murphy wore them on the *Dumplin'* red carpet, and I died.)

Whatever Nicole Byer is wearing on *Nailed It!*

Gwynnie Bee

Dia & Co

—Lily Anderson

Ava & Viv

Original Use

Both are Target brands that—while **Original Use** is not inclusive of folks above 2XL—make clothes that actually fit a body well, no matter what shape or size. Plus, both are very affordable and (while my sense of style is very tacky) very fashionable!

—Mason Deaver

Swak Design

Lane Bryant

Eleven60

Ava & Viv

Jibri online

—Renée Watson

Torrid: Available at most malls, has good clearance deals usually, often has coupons.

Hot Topic: Available at most malls, sometimes has surprisingly good stuff in larger sizes; can be a bit expensive, but they often run sales.

ModCloth: Online retailer; possibly out of the price range of many teens, but they run good sales every now and then.

eShakti: Online retailer; sometimes runs sales, has HUGE selection of customization and size options—highly recommend if people are looking for a nice, as-close-to-tailored-as-you-can-get-online dress.

Figleaves: Online retailer; I haven't purchased from them, but I hear good things about their bra selection—as a teen I had the hardest time finding bras that fit from standard retailers like Victoria's Secret!

Hips & Curves: Online retailer; I haven't ordered from them either, but I hear good things about their bra and underwear selection.

Buffalo Exchange: Available at several locations; it's a trendy used-clothing store, so the selection can be hit-or-miss depending on local clientele, but they do a good job of picking out good items, so the selection is a bit more stylish than Goodwill while the prices remain affordable. I wouldn't call it a plus-size retailer, though, just a treasure-hunt option.

Old Navy: Brick and mortar locations seem to typically only go up to size 18 or so, but I think they've got a larger selection online, and their pants are pretty solid and affordable. I have sacrificed many Old Navy pants to the altar of chub rub, haha.

Target: Their plus selection is increasingly stylish, and their shorts and pants have been on point lately. I personally have a harder time finding bottoms than tops, so anywhere that has solid pants is a godsend for me. Plus, if you're on the border between straight sizes and plus sizes, they have some great options for that range.

—*S. Qiouyi Lu*

Acknowledgments

I would be lost without the endless love and support of my husband, William Tucker. You're the velociraptor of my heart, honey, and I love your face. This book wouldn't exist without the friendship and constant support of Angelo Muredda, who so many years ago told me, "It's OK to get mad." Thanks for always being mad with me, Angelo.

I have been sustained and buoyed throughout my life by my friends and family. There are too many of you to list, but I have to specifically mention a few. My sister, Gina Manfredi, my best blood friend. My best besties, throughout it all: Whitney Holland, Elliot Williams, and Mike Doidge. My legendary library girls: Ashley McLendon, Heather Moore, Karen Rowell, Lori Schexnayder, and Erin Waller. My Raton crew, thirty years and counting: Daniel Esquibel, Dave Pacheco, Rainbeaux Trujillo, and Dori Yob Kilmer. And of course all my #DiversityJedi—who make me do the work.

This all started with Twitter—can you imagine? This book began because of a dream and a tweet from Dahlia Adler; I am forever in her debt. Thank you also to Tess Sharpe and Preeti Chhibber for their eyes on this at the very beginning. And I am thankful for my agent and old pal, Barry Goldblatt, who believes in my voice and also laughs at the same stuff as me. That's really important.

The book you are holding looks so amazing due in no small part to the unerring eyes of Hana Anouk Nakamura and Lisa Tegtmeier; I am grateful for their brilliance. And you wouldn't be holding this book at all without the work and energy poured into it by Jessica Gotz and my editor, Anne Heltzel. Anne believed in this book from the beginning, and I am grateful she saw LARGE things in me and this title.

Finally: thank you to every fat contributor in this book, for walking this road and holding a hand out. And to every fat person who has put on the crop top, walked a red carpet, kept their head up high in the face of jeers, who has fought for their dignity, even in quiet ways, you have made all this possible.

Author and Illustrator Copyrights